About the Author

Ronald Bonewitz originally trained as a geologist and has consulted on archaeological excavations in the western United States. He has travelled widely in Yucatán visiting Maya ruins, and explored unmapped Maya sites on the sacred island of Cozumel. He is a founder of the New Millennium Church, an interfaith church and holds a PhD in Behavioural Science. He has lectured widely on personal development around the world and is the author of several books on natural philosophy and personal development including *The Story of the Findhorn Crystals*, *The Pulse of Life: Understanding Your Life through the Rhythms of Nature*, *The Crystal Heart: Healing the Heart Centre* and *The Timeless Wisdom of Ancient Egypt*. He lives in the south of England.

Maya Prophecy

Piatkus Guides

A PIATKUS GUIDE

Maya Prophecy

Dr Ronald Bonewitz

PIATKUS

To the living Maya and their struggle
to maintain their cultural heritage

© 1999 Dr Ronald Bonewitz

First published in 1999 by
Judy Piatkus (Publishers) Ltd
5 Windmill Street, London W1P 1HF

ISBN 0-7499-1959-0

Typeset by Action Publishing Technology Limited, Gloucester
Printed & bound in Great Britain by
Mackays of Chatham PLC

Contents

Acknowledgements

Special thanks are again due to Guy and Meriel Ballard, Godfrey Thomas and, as always, to Lilian Verner-Bonds. I also thank my commissioning editor, Sandra Rigby, for many helpful suggestions about the organisation of the material, and Gina Llewellyn, for her prompt and efficient typing.

Guide to Pronunciation

It is difficult to reproduce accurately words and names in the Maya tongue. Their spelling has been passed to us through their original transliteration into 16th-century Spanish. Certain sounds in Maya do not exist in Spanish, just as certain sounds in Spanish do not exist in English. To further complicate matters, English has very different pronunciations both regionally and internationally.

Listed below are a number of pronunciations that vary from the English pronunciation. For those letters not listed, pronounce them as in English.

☆ **A** is always pronounced as in **a**we.

☆ **B** is always pronounced as in **b**ank.

☆ **C** is always pronounced like a k as in **c**at. For example, the Spanish word for house, *casa*, is pronounced kawsa (remember the 'a' sound from above).

☆ **CH** is pronounced as in **ch**oo-choo.

☆ **E** at the end of a word is always pronounced as an a, as in r**ay**. In the middle of a word it is pronounced like the e in sh**e**ll.

☆ **I** is pronounced ee as in p**i**zza.

☆ **J** is pronounced as a w, for example, Jaurez is [Wa <u>ress</u>].

☆ **L** is always pronounced as in she**ll**.

☆ **M** is always pronounced as in **M**ary.

☆ **P** is as in **p**apa.

☆ **Q** is always pronounced as a k, as in **k**ing.

☆ **T** as in **t**ea.

☆ **U** is pronounced as a w, as in **w**ater.

☆ **X** at the beginning of a word is pronounced as a ts sound. At the end of a word it is pronounced like h, as in **h**unt. So Mexico is [May-<u>he</u>-ko]; Ix Chel is [Ih Chell].

☆ **Z** is always pronounced like the s in **s**ee and written in translation as ss.

Here are some other Maya words and names that appear in the text. The emphasis should be placed on the underlined syllable.

Chac	[Chawk]
Chichén Itzá	[Chee-chen Eet-sah]
Copán	[Ko-pawn]
Itzamná	[Eet-sawm nah]
Ix Chel	[Ih Chell]
Kinich Ahau	[Kin-eech Awe-how]
Kukulcan	[Koo-cool-kawn]
Pacal	[Pah-kawl]
Palenque	[Paw-len-kay]
Pauahtun	[Pa-wah-tun]
Popul Vuh	[Po-pull Vuh]
Quetzalcoatl	[Kate-tsal-ko-wahu-tull]
Quiché	[Kee-shay]
Uaxactún	[Wah-hoc-tun]
Viracocha	[Veera-coacha]
Xbalanque	[Tsblawn-kay]
Yucatán	[Yoo-kuh-tahn]

Introduction

When the opportunity to write a book on the Maya Prophecy presented itself, I leaped at the chance. It is, for me, a culmination of many years of interest, not just in the Maya and in prophecy, but in a broad interweaving of separate strands from apparently unrelated cultures, across both time and space. I grew up in the Southwest of the United States, and an interest in the native cultures from further south in Mexico and Central America came naturally. In my teens I read extensively about the Aztecs, Incas and, of course, the Maya. I was thrilled to discover that my father had been sent some Aztec artefacts by one of his teachers, who had excavated sites in Mexico in the 1920s.

I studied geology at university, with secondary training in archaeology. From time to time I was consulted on the geological aspects of archaeological digs in the American Southwest. Later, as a professional pilot, I often flew into the Yucatán peninsula, and visited Maya sites. I gazed into the forbidding cenote, the sacred well of sacrifice at Chichén Itzá, and watched the sunrise from the tops of pyramids. And I had the extreme good fortune to be befriended by several living Maya on the then serene island of Cozumel, and I was taken to unrecorded and unexcavated Maya ruins.

Later, when I became involved in personal development and spiritual teaching, I came to know a recognised living prophet, Revd Paul Solomon. I was familiar with the work of the celebrated prophet Edgar Cayce and was pleased to discover my previous books were held in the Cayce Library in Virginia Beach, Virginia. I was equally fortunate to participate in the filming of part of a television series on modern prophets. Thus, with the growing interest in the Maya Prophecy, the time for this book was just right.

In this book I have tried to sort out carefully what is factually known, what is reasonable interpretation, and what is speculation. Issues here may well concern literally every living person on the planet – and not a few yet to be born – so it is important to be as clear as possible.

This is a book about a worried people. Let's cast their worries in modern terms: suppose we knew that every 5,000 years, the Earth passed through a cloud of comets and usually collided with at least one of them. The result: a planetwide catastrophe, with entire nations obliterated, whole species wiped out and the human population decimated. Civilisations collapse, and the world is plunged back into the Stone Age. Add to this a belief that offering everything – literally our lives – to the gods, might forestall or prevent the catastrophe. Wouldn't we do all that we could to prevent it if we could? Would any effort be too large, any sacrifice be too great if it could be averted?

But this is precisely the sort of catastrophe the Maya believed themselves to be facing, and – if their prophecies are to be believed – they and we still may face. What sets the Maya Prophecy aside from others are its antiquity, with roots long before the Maya themselves, and its mathematical precision, an accuracy that the Maya inherited from a much older civilisation and refined and modified to an even greater degree. Its meaning for those living today is the subject of this book.

But what of the Maya themselves? The Maya are most commonly associated with the grisly horrors of human sacrifice. Stories abound of sacred ball games played with the severed heads of sacrificed victims – and worse. Was this just blood thirstiness? Maybe it was a willing sacrifice in the hope of averting an even greater disaster for the whole of the Maya nation – and is this any less than a modern soldier is willing to do? Seen in the perspective of the Maya Prophecy, a whole new light is cast on the Maya culture, including its apparently less appealing features. This new perspective will help us to understand the urgency and the reality of the Prophecy, and why it remains relevant.

This book explores various dimensions of Maya life and belief systems to determine the relevancy of the Prophecy. We can gain important insights into our own lives, as well as indications of how we, too, should be preparing for the events of the Prophecy, should they come to pass. Examination of other ancient civilisations also reveals evidence of the events that the Maya believe preceded the last catastrophe. Startling confirmation can be found in biblical accounts and the writings and beliefs of other peoples half a world away from the Maya.

Beyond their unsavoury reputation for human sacrifice, the Maya still have a deep and ancient understanding of the Oneness of all creation expressed in their thought and religion. It appears that human sacrifice may have been relatively uncommon during the earliest periods of Maya development, including the peak of Maya civilisation, possibly becoming more widespread only after the Toltec invasion of the

Northern Maya and the incorporation of many Toltec beliefs into Maya life. The Prophecy was a part of Maya life from the beginning of Maya civilisation, and predates the Toltec invasion by many hundreds of years. So the emphasis in this book is on the Classic Period of the Maya, when Maya civilisation culminated in the south, long before the Toltec influences. By that time many universal archetypes had been incorporated into Maya beliefs.

Guided Visualisations

This book includes meditations, visualisations and exercises to connect the reader experientially to the ancient knowledge of the Maya. Their beliefs and lives were intimately linked with the great pattern of life, in many respects in more ways than modern man. These exercises use Maya sacred imagery, which incorporates universal archetypes as relevant today as they were then.

Some readers will have no experience of either visualisation or meditation, which are simply forms of relaxation. The images suggested in each visualisation are carefully chosen to stimulate that portion of one's being that identifies with the archetypes expressed through Maya life. These are universal, and part of everyone, touching on dimensions of existence that are rarely accessed through life in the 'normal' world, where much has been forgotten. These visualisations help reawaken that which has been lost, that which sustained and enriched the lives of not only the Maya but peoples everywhere. To our great loss, the modern world has been deprived of much of our deepest heritage. Many social problems and upheavals that surround us in no small measure result from this. There are numerous ways to recover that which has been lost, and what is offered here is but a small portion. It is a very rich source. It nurtured the peoples of Mesoamerica for at least 3,000 years, and continues to do so today.

Past Lives

The archetypes used in our guided imagery of the ancient Maya are universal and timeless. They may trigger past-life memories for some readers, but be assured that nothing in this book requires a belief in reincarnation. Of those readers who have experienced past-life memories, some will remember a life among the Maya, or one of the other related Mesoamerican peoples – the Toltecs, Olmecs, Aztecs or the Inca in Peru. This is fairly likely, because, if you think of it, 3,000 years of human history happened in Mesoamerica, so it would be more surprising if you did not recall a life from then.

It cannot be emphasised too strongly: the point of past-life work is not about remembering past lives, but about remembering their unfinished lessons. Life is about learning, whether in this life or others. There is a temptation to get hung-up on past lives: 'I-was-so-and-so.' Forget it. The important thing is to recall what was the lesson of being so-and-so. The Maya understand the body as a vehicle for movement into what is beyond. Learning to live in the body and still be fully connected to the source of your being is ultimately life's only lesson.

EXERCISE: PREPARING FOR VISUALISATION AND MEDITATION

It is important in each exercise to complete the steps in the order given.

☆ *Creating a sacred space:* For the ancient Maya the whole world was a sacred place. Our modern lives have become so intense, practical and materialistic in their orientation that the claims of the moment are so great we hardly know where we are. Creating a personal sacred space is an absolute necessity. It is a space where you meditate, or where you can simply experience and bring forth what you are and what you might be. It might be a room, or a certain hour or so in the day, some music that you really love, or a place out of doors, but it is a space in which you feel a connection to life in the way that the ancients regarded the world in which they lived. It is a place of creative incubation.

☆ *Get comfortable:* Sitting is the best position for meditation. You can meditate lying down, though it can be easy to fall asleep! If sitting on the floor, arrange your legs in the most comfortable position; if sitting on a chair, keep your legs uncrossed and your feet flat on the floor to create the best connection to the earth's energy. Keep your back as straight as possible, and fold your hands comfortably in your lap.

☆ *Breathe:* Take a deep breath, and exhale slowly. Do this several times. Relax and focus on the rise and fall of your chest. Your eyes will close of their own accord, and your breathing will become shallow. This relaxation technique is good for dealing with stress, and can be used at any time, even in the office.

☆ *Visualisation:* When you are relaxed, you can start the suggested visualisation. Always remember that you are in complete control of your experience and can stop at any time. This is not hypnosis or anything similar: it is just relaxation.

☆ *Be a Maya:* You may wish to take the visualisations a step further, and add some extra dimensions of Maya thought to the process. In a sense, you may become your own Maya priest. They interpreted the omens as a combination of astrologer, psychic and shaman, one in communion with all of nature. The Maya usually divined at night, when the gods were believed to be closer. This does not mean that visualisations cannot be done during the day, or that it is necessary to set your alarm for 3 am!

☆ *Direction:* The Maya, in common with many native peoples, have a firm belief that the cardinal directions possess distinct characteristics relevant to life. When doing the visualisations, try to face in the direction the Maya would prescribe for such an undertaking.

North is associated with death by the Maya, though it must be understood that death to the Maya did not mean a cessation of life, rather it was the means by which life transformed itself from one state into another. North is also the direction through which the ancestral dead influenced the living. In modern terms, we might say it is related to the inner issues created from our past experiences with parents or our early carers. These were, in turn, usually created for them by their parents, and so on – definitely showing the influence of our ancestors!

East, the direction of the rising sun, brings heat, fire and life into the world. With visualisations seeking answers to enliven and enrich your life or introducing something new, face east. But remember that east is also the direction of sacrifice, reminding you that all things in this world have a price; in order to receive something, you may have to give up something else.

West is the direction of entry for goodness and wisdom. If you are seeking an answer to a specific problem, or a resolution to a thorny question, face west while visualising. The aspect of goodness is equally important, and the wisdom being sought must reflect the highest wisdom: all that comes into your life should reflect the highest ideals and purposes of that life.

South is the direction of the day, of light, of daily life, with all the mundane activities that were a natural part of the spiritual life. The Maya knew that all life was spiritual; indeed, it is not known whether they even had a word such as 'spiritual'. We only give something a name when we can perceive it as separate from other things. Every living moment for the Maya was 'spiritual'. We name it. They lived it.

1

The Maya and the Prophecy

It may seem strange to begin a book on Maya Prophecy by stating that in the strictest sense the Maya Prophecy is neither Maya nor prophecy. This Mesoamerican civilisation was but the inheritor of a body of information that includes within it a forecast of a coming event. We may be grateful to the Maya for its faithful preservation.

So, does this in any way invalidate or discredit this information? Far from it. In fact, as you will discover, it gives it a validity and an urgency that requires very serious attention.

This book sets out to answer the fundamental questions about the Prophecy:

☆ What is the Prophecy?

☆ Is it true?

☆ Does it apply to you?

☆ What can you do about it?

It is also important to establish why the Prophecy is not really a prophecy, and why it is something much more substantial.

All of Maya life was rooted in prediction: not just of long-term cycles, but also of everyday events. Maya astronomers observed and calculated the daily movement of the planets, especially Venus, and made predictions and forecasts based on their supposed interaction with the gods who ruled the various days of the Maya calendar. It was, in fact, not far removed from modern astrology, except that an entire culture revolved around it. Virtually every aspect of life was based on the prognostications of the priests, from the major decisions of the rulers down to the smallest activities of the lowest subject. When we extract a single prediction and label it the Maya Prophecy, we are taking it out of context, and without re-establishing that context we have no hope whatever of understanding the Prophecy.

But what, precisely, *is* foretold?

The Prophecy says that the world goes through a series of cycles, each one called a 'Sun' by the Maya (and also by the Aztecs, who shared a similar cosmology). At the end of each Sun, the world experiences a cataclysm, civilisation collapses, and a new mankind evolves. The Maya believed — and still believe, though they are supposedly 'Christianised' — that there have been four Suns. We are now in the period of the Fifth Sun, which began in 3114 BC. The Fifth Sun is due to end in AD 2012. On 23 December, to be precise.

Is there any reason to take such a prediction seriously? Isn't it merely a quaint relic of ancient mythology, without relevance in the modern, scientific world? As we will discover in the chapters that follow, there is good reason to believe that it may be a great deal more than a myth, and that we should take it very seriously indeed. Without knowing exactly what it was they were preserving, it appears that the

Maya have passed down knowledge of the 5,000-year returns of a long-period comet that wreaks havoc on the world at each return.

The events described in various Maya and New World sources are entirely consistent with the effects of such an impact. And archaeological evidence from a number of places around the world also supports it. And, while evidence is missing or as yet unrecognised for the end of the Third Sun, the ends of the First and Second Suns are well enough attested by climatic evidence: the decline and then the abrupt end of the last Ice Age.

Who Were the Maya?

The Maya were a varied and mixed culture whose homeland lay in the highland and lowland areas of Guatemala, Honduras, and the southern portion of Mexico, called Yucatán. Along with the rest of Mexico, this area is known as Mesoamerica. Between about 2000 BC and AD 250, the Maya came increasingly under the influence of outside cultures, principally from the north, and farming and intensive settlement began in earnest. Cities eventually began to develop, large public works such as temples and pyramids were constructed, and writing, numbers, and the calendar – with its attendant astronomy and astrology – became established throughout the region.

While most shared a common core religious belief, the Maya were in fact a group of individual cultures. At the time of the Spanish conquest, the Maya spoke some 30 different languages, some as similar as British and American English, and some as different as English and French. There were further regional variations in culture, world-view and economics, and politically there was no central organisation

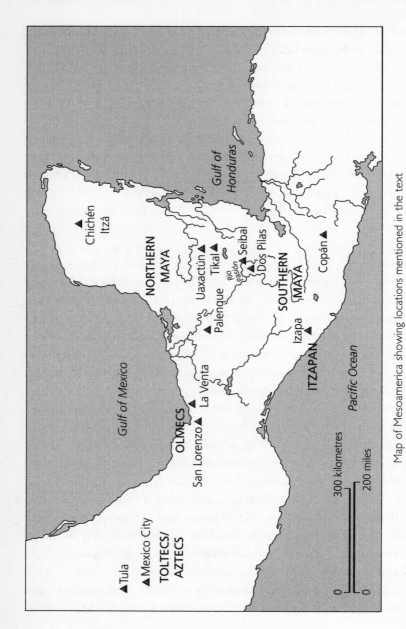

Map of Mesoamerica showing locations mentioned in the text

at all. There was no central king figure like Montezuma, king of the politically unified Aztecs further north, and there was never a single Maya nation, as with the Aztecs. The Maya lived in a series of city-states, often bitter enemies of one another, each with its own local variations on the basic beliefs. Each city and its surrounding area was a political entity unto itself, at certain times co-operating with others and at other times at war. Also, it must be understood that the Maya of one historical period are not the Maya of a later historical period.

As with all cultures, there were developments, gains, and losses over history. When we discover that Maya are living today in southern Mexico, appearing to retain the ancient culture to some degree, we also know that the influences of Spanish culture and their uprooting from their traditional habitats have also changed their culture beyond recognition to an ancient Maya. As with the ancient Maya, each group of modern Maya have a culture more or less independent from the others, with similarities and differences. Indeed, linguists recognise more than 24 distinct living Maya languages, some of them unintelligible to the others.

When we begin to study the world-view of the Maya that led to the Maya Prophecy, we therefore need to understand that there is no single, all-encompassing Maya world-view. Beliefs varied from region to region and changed over time. A core cosmology and system of symbols was central to each of the varying Maya beliefs and shared with virtually all of the Mesoamerican groups of Mexico and Central America, including the Aztecs, Toltecs and the Mixtecs. And it is from this central view that we are able to begin understanding the Prophecy.

But before examining these core beliefs in the following chapters, let us first look into the history of the Maya, for here we begin to move backwards toward the origin of the Prophecy itself.

Origins of the Maya

All of the available archaeological evidence shows that the areas occupied by the Maya had not been previously inhabited. Asian in origin, and filtering down through North America, their ancestors originally crossed into Alaska over the land bridge that existed between Asia and North America when sea levels were lower at the end of the last Ice Age. The Maya book the *Popol Vuh* may even record the original land-bridge crossing, handed down through oral tradition:

> It isn't clear how they crossed over the sea. They crossed over as if there were no sea. They just crossed over on some stones, stones piled up in the sand. And they gave it a name: Stones Courses, Sand Banks was their name for the place where they crossed through the midst of the sea. Where the waters were divided, they crossed over.

Spreading across the region by 7500 BC, the settlers were essentially hunters, but farming and agricultural villages were well established through much of the Maya area by 1500 BC.

The Olmecs

To the west and north of the Maya, on the Gulf Coast, by 1500 BC the Olmecs had already long possessed a complex and well-developed culture, from which the Maya directly inherited the Prophecy. Most archaeologists consider the Olmecs to be the 'mother culture' of Central America. The greatest mystery surrounding the Olmecs is where they themselves came from. There is no evidence of a developmental phase anywhere in Mexico, nor anywhere else in the

New World for that matter. Nigel Davis, author of *The Ancient Kingdoms of Mexico*, states that: 'The proto Olmec phase remains an enigma.' Equally, there is no real evidence about exactly who the Olmec were. Not a single Olmec skeleton has been discovered. Even the name Olmec is assigned to them by archaeologists; we have no idea even what they called themselves. And yet whoever these people were, they appear to be the foundation upon which all of the later civilisations of Mesoamerica were built.

It is suggested that this culture dates back more than 3,000 years. Like the Toltecs further north, the Olmecs were great mathematicians, astronomers and architects; unlike the Toltecs, the Olmecs practised human sacrifice. It is clear that later cultures venerated the Olmecs. The Aztecs, who occupied the same lands as the earlier Toltecs, collected ancient Olmec ritual objects and placed them in positions of importance in Aztec temples. The centre of Aztec and Toltec culture was around the current location of Mexico City; Olmec culture was situated further south and east along the Gulf coast, around the town of Coatzecoalcos.

The oldest known Olmec site is in San Lorenzo in Veracruz. Here sophisticated and well-developed forms of pottery, sculpture and carving were discovered. The Olmecs had constructed an artificial mound more than 100 feet high, 4,000 feet long and 2,000 feet wide, as well as over 20 artificial reservoirs linked by stone-lined conduits. By 1000 BC the city had been destroyed by unknown forces, but its influence had already spread throughout the whole of Mesoamerica, with the exception, initially, of the Maya domain.

The other major Olmec site is at La Venta, on an island in the Tonala River. It was a highly sophisticated centre, with extensive public buildings, tombs and temples, an elaborate cosmology and well-developed art forms. In the ceremonial heart of La Venta were two pyramids, one of stone and the other a fluted cone of packed earth, 100 feet tall and about 200 feet in diameter, consisting of ten flutes. The pyramids occupied either end of a central axis, along which were aligned several smaller pyramids, plazas, platforms and mounds, covering a total area of more than 3 square miles.

One of the most startling discoveries at La Venta before its recent destruction by the oil industry, was a stela (a standing stone), 14 feet high, 7 feet wide and almost 3 feet thick. Its carvings showed two men, both dressed in elaborate robes and wearing shoes with turned up toes. One of the figures was deliberately defaced, but the second depicted a Caucasian male with a high-bridged nose, and a long flowing beard. Two other stones, also depicting Caucasian figures, were also found there. The earliest Mesoamerican stories of the 'god' Quetzalcoatl, the 'bearded white man from across the sea' who brought civilisation to Mesoamerica, were handed down from the Olmecs. So do these carvings form a representation of him? How could the Olmecs have guessed at the racial features of a Caucasian?

Within a few centuries the Olmec influence of La Venta began to be felt within the Maya world, as shown in surviving relics of their material culture, such as pottery. Their style of monumental art and architecture had yet to be adopted, perhaps because the Maya had not established a sufficient cultural base to support such labour-intensive works. But it is likely that during this period the calendar and mathematics were passed to the Maya from the Olmecs – along with the Prophecy.

There is some evidence, in fact, that the transfer of knowledge from the Olmec to the Maya was not a direct one, but that a third culture served as an intermediary between the two. This was the Izapan civilisation, which occupied a geographical space and time between the Olmec and the Maya. The earliest inscriptions using dates of the Maya Long Count calendar have been located in Izapan sites, the earliest dating to AD 36, nearly 350 years before the oldest Maya site date. It is thought that the Izapan and the Maya co-existed for a period of time, before the Izapan disappeared. Whether they were absorbed by the Maya or disappeared totally is unknown.

The Maya were drawing on one or both of these ancient cultures in the foundations of their own culture. Their calendar, mathematics, and architecture were thus not Mayan at all, but a legacy from an older culture, along with their essential beliefs about the nature of the world and its cyclic destructions.

The Rise of the Maya

The Maya can be divided into essentially two periods based on their geographical location: the Southern Maya and the Northern Maya.

The Southern Maya world was located in the southern part of the Yucatán Peninsula, in present-day Honduras and Guatemala and the Mexican states of Chiapas and Tabasco. The time of its habitation is subdivided into three periods by some archaeologists.

The beginning of the **Early Period** is undated. It ends in AD 374, the date of the oldest known sculpture in a purely Maya setting, though Maya-style ceramics and sculptures a couple of centuries older have also been found. The oldest city is Uaxactún, on the northern border of present-day Guatemala. Other major cities included Tikal and Naranjo, close to Uaxactún, and further south, Copán in Honduras. The **Middle Period** is generally considered to be AD 374–472. The major city of Palenque was founded during this period. The border between the Mexican states Chiapas and Tabasco also serves as the boundary between the position of the Southern Maya civilisation and the later Northern Maya civilisation.

The **Classic Period**, which by some definitions also includes the Middle Period, lasted from AD 472–800, during which time the cities of Seibal, Ixkun and Flores were constructed. By AD 800 both the Classic Period and the Southern Maya civilisation came to an end. Within a relatively short span of time it had virtually abandoned its cities and moved 250 miles to the north. The Northern Maya lived in the northern part of the Yucatán Peninsula and their cities were built on land in entirely virgin jungle, the most famous being Chichén Itzá. They took with them their religion, their beliefs and the Prophecy, leaving the cities of the south to be reclaimed by the jungle.

Maya Social Structure

The Maya were essentially city-dwellers. The Maya ruling classes – the nobility and the priesthood – lived in the cities, bases for all authority, culture, and spiritual activity. Compared to European cultures, even under feudalism, Maya social structure was much more divided. There was no middle class, and the extremes of status were severe indeed.

Nobles and priests lived in lavish palaces and temples, mostly built on high ground and often fortress-like in character. As they were few in number, and the vast majority of Maya lived in poor conditions, the nobility had good reason to wall themselves up in fortresses. The nobility were very exclusive, calling themselves the *Almehenob* ('those who have fathers and mothers'), meaning those who could boast of a genealogy. A further group in the noble class – called the

Halac Uinicil, meaning 'the true man' or 'the real thing' — were hereditary rulers and princes. Members of the priest-hood also came from the nobility. Evidence suggests that during the Classic Period religious and ritual duties were performed by the elite — the rulers, nobility and scribes. The priesthood as a separate institution appears to have been a late introduction from the Toltecs.

The rest of the people, the vast majority, were farmers and artisans. The farmer gave a third of his harvest to the nobility, a third to the priests, and was allowed to keep only the other remaining third for himself. In Europe, the medieval tenth, or tithe, was considered excessive and ulti-mately led to uprisings and revolts. It is possible that by keeping the populous generally underfed, revolt was prevented simply because people did not have the energy to mount a rebellion.

Maya cities, just as European cities, were not viable without the farmers who supported them. The staple food of the Mayas was maize, grown in the *milpas*, burned-out spaces in the jungle where Maya cities came to be built. Milpa farming is still common in the Maya highlands of Mexico, following ancient patterns: it begins with the clearing and burning of an area of forest (the ash serves as fertiliser for the new crop). Once the planting is ready to begin, a Maya priest performs a ceremony to placate the modern Maya god called the Earth Owner, who controls the clouds, rains and wind. Shrines are often set up in the corners and the centre of the fields, where farmers offer prayers, candles, flowers and pine boughs. Into the same hole as the maize seeds may be planted seeds of beans and squash, which will grow as ground cover beneath the developing maize. Other plants, such as gourds and chillies, are planted around the edge of the milpa.

Wild animals, important in the Maya diet, as well as for

ritual purposes, included deer, rabbits and wild turkey, and even rats, mice and iguanas. A number of wild plants were also collected, such as coconut, mango, papaya, guava and cacao, which was used to make the drink chocolate.

Between sowing and harvest the farmer, along with all his slaves, engaged in building construction. Because there were no carts or draft animals, every stone of every building was wrestled from the quarry to its building site by hand. It is likely that the priests' third of the harvest was set aside for the labour necessary for huge building projects. Given the impressive architectural and astronomical accomplishments of the Maya civilisation, it is remarkable that it failed to develop some of the most fundamental tools that had appeared centuries earlier in the rest of the world: the plough and the wheel. The explanation for this is quite simple: the entire focus of the Maya civilisation was not on the earth, but on the skies. It was not built around the daily lives of its inhabitants, but was focused on the single underlying belief upon which the entire civilisation was built: the Maya Prophecy.

The world of the Maya has recently received a great deal of attention in both scientific circles and the popular press. A number of books have attributed all manner of esoteric wisdom to the ancient Maya. Even if such understanding was present, *which* Maya possessed it? Our general image of the Maya is the same as 13th- or 14th-century Europeans: a small minority ruling class, perhaps no more than 2–3 per cent of the population, who were well educated, literate and the possessors of the 'highest' knowledge of their culture. The vast majority were illiterate peasants, locked into their lifestyle by their culture and their position in society defined by birth, essentially servile to the tiny ruling group. When we speak of the enlightenment of the Maya culture – or indeed that of other ancient cultures such as Egypt or Sumeria — we are speaking of societies where the highest sacred knowledge was not shared by the ordinary man or woman but reserved for an elite. Modern concepts of enlightenment oblige the possessors of higher knowledge to strive to pass on some of their wisdom to the masses, and not just reserve it principally for themselves.

In assessing the esoteric knowledge possessed by a culture, there is much that can be determined and much that can be reasonably interpreted from what is preserved. But we must be exceedingly careful not to base our interpretations on our modern understanding. We must attempt to put ourselves in the minds of the Maya, especially when interpreting the Maya Prophecy. Most of what we know about the Prophecy is preserved in the surviving Maya books.

Maya Books

Maya Books in Maya Hieroglyphics

The Maya possessed a highly sophisticated written language, and wrote extensively on a wide range of topics.

In what might today be termed 'cultural genocide', when the Spanish arrived in the mid-16th century, they set about deliberately destroying the entire culture of Mexico and Central America. The Spanish quickly recognised that the writing of the Maya was an essential part of both their culture and their belief system, and realised that by destroying their books and their pictorial art, they would destroy much of Maya culture. A 16th-century Spanish bishop, Diego de Landa, put it very succinctly: 'We found a large number of books in these characters [hieroglyphics] and, as they contained nothing in which there were not to be seen superstition and lies of the devil, we burned them all, which they regretted to an amazing degree, and which caused them much affliction.' Among the books destroyed by the Spanish were genealogies, biographies, collections of songs, science books, history, prophecy, astrology and ritual. Juan De Zumarraga, the first archbishop of Mexico, boasted of destroying 500 temples, 20,000 idols and tens of thousands of books. Another Spanish bishop, Fray Deigo De Landa was a particular persecutor of Maya culture. In a single night in the Yucatán town of Mani, south of Mérida, virtually the entire written culture of the Maya was consumed in one huge bonfire. Hundreds and perhaps thousands of years of written records disappeared in a matter of hours. It was a tragedy comparable to the burning of the great library in Alexandria in Egypt.

Thanks to the misplaced zeal of these early Spaniards, we are left with only four remaining Maya books written in Maya hieroglyphics: the Paris Codex, the Dresden Codex, the Madrid Codex and the recently discovered Grolier Codex. Each book consists of a long strip of bark-paper, folded like an accordion. Both sides of the paper were coated with a thin layer of white plaster, upon which were painted pictures and symbols. All four of the surviving books were painted just before the Spanish conquest and deal with religious and scientific matters. Their content is devoted largely to divination. Among them is an astronomical table for the movements of Venus, a table of eclipses and possible references to the movements of other planets. Most of the emphasis is astrological, containing statements specifying the relationship between time, space and deities.

The Paris Codex was discovered in a waste-paper basket in the Library of Paris in 1859! This 11 page document contains an account of Maya history. The Dresden Codex, concerned with the Maya cycles of time, appeared in 1939, when an unknown seller passed the manuscript to the director of the Dresden Library in Germany. Librarian Ernst Forstemann studied the manuscript for many years, and discovered the fact that the current Maya calendar started in 3114 BC. Also described in the Codex were solar eclipses, stories of Quetzalcoatl and Maya ceremonies. The Madrid Codex is the combination of a 70-page document and a 42-page document, both of which were found gathering dust in Estramadura, Spain.

Aside from the remaining books, there is a wealth of Maya inscription, carved on monuments and structures and painted on pottery. Until very recently the assumption has been that those inscriptions also dealt with religious subjects, as did the surviving texts. In fact for the most part their subject matter is concerned with dynastic history.

Maya Books in Spanish Script

Much of our understanding of the Maya universe is based on Spanish-language documents from the early colonial period, when a few enlightened Spaniards managed to save something from the general conflagration of Maya knowledge demanded by the Church. Archaeological evidence confirms much of this knowledge and extends our understanding. Further, because Maya beliefs were shared to a degree with the Aztecs further north, much can be inferred as Spaniards did more to preserve Aztec knowledge and cultural beliefs.

The Spanish were impressed with the Aztecs principally because of their wealth in gold and silver. Because the Maya were not so rich in those metals, the Spanish dismissed them as 'poor'. Their gold- and religion-induced blindness prevented the Spanish from seeing that the Maya were, in fact, culturally much richer than the Aztecs. Even the few 16th-century Spanish commentaries on Maya culture – one of which was even written in co-operation with a living Maya priest – went virtually unnoticed until the 19th century. Fortunately these few writings provided some essential clues as interest in the Maya was reawakened.

It is not until this last decade that real strides have been made in unravelling the Maya script. One of the principal barriers has been an uncertainty about which of the Maya languages was recorded in each of the four surviving texts. No modern ones are the same as the languages in the texts. Along with all other facets of their culture, they have undergone enormous change in the last 500 years.

One of the richest sources of historical information about the Mayas and the Toltecs whose culture infused the Northern Maya is a native prince by the name of Ixtlilxochitl, baptised into the Catholic church and a well-educated man. Writing shortly after the Spanish conquest, he began to sketch out the history of his people, particularly their traditions, going back to the very earliest days of history when the supposedly legendary city of Tula (now recognised as the present-day Mexican city of Tollan) was founded by the Toltec people. The early Toltecs knew how to write, do mathematics, make calendars, and build great palaces and temples. (Ixtlilxochitl, of course, had no idea that the Toltecs derived these skills from the Olmecs.) The early rulers of Tula were also renowned for their wisdom; their laws were just, and their religion was mild and free from the cruelties of later eras. According to Ixtlilxochitl, this lasted about 500 years, and was followed by famine, civil war and quarrels between the ruling dynasties. Toltec survivors migrated to Tabasco and later Yucatán, where they conquered the Maya, who had at about the same time shifted their culture from the south to the north. The magnificent city of Chichén Itzá, founded at this time, shows a considerable fusion of Toltec and Maya.

Ixtlilxochitl wrote his chronicles in the 16th century. When they were rediscovered in the 19th century they were assumed to be mythical, but archaeological discoveries since 1940 have demonstrated their accuracy. Tula was located, and within it were pyramids and well-preserved reliefs and fine sculptures. Ixtlilxochitl's writing has even encouraged some archaeologists to believe that the Toltecs, rather than the Olmecs, were the cultural ancestors of the Maya which may in fact be the case for the Northern Maya, who were conquered by them.

These books provide a basic understanding of the Maya world-view, and the thought processes that caused them to embrace so thoroughly the Prophecy and its implications.

The Popol Vuh

The *Popol Vuh* is the prime source for the Maya cosmology, setting forth the idea of the cycle of 'Suns'. Its survival across the centuries is a remarkable story. Early in the 18th century a Dominican monk, Father Francisco Ximenez, accidentally stumbled upon an old manuscript, hidden behind some loose stones in the wall of his church, Santo Tomas Castenango. He had won the confidence of the local Indians, who were Quiché Maya, living in Guatemala and Honduras and speaking the Quiché tongue. The book's unknown writers attempted to set down the ancient traditions and history of the Quiché, the very first line stating: 'The *Popol Vuh* cannot be seen any more . . . the original book written long ago existed, but its sight is hidden from the searcher and the thinker.' Thus the text we currently know by that name is not the original Maya book, but rather one probably written from memory. This does not necessarily negate its value, as oral tradition is known to have existed in civilisations like the Maya and is often highly accurate in its recollection of ancient events.

The sacred book of the Quiché contains the Maya creation story, the history of the Quiché people, and the stories of two sets of twins who bear a remarkable resemblance to the Egyptian myths of Isis and Osiris, Seth and Nephthys. It is properly called the *Book of Counsel*, and it is the book a Maya priest would refer to in the same way as a Christian priest would consult his Bible for counsel. Composed in the alphabetic version of Maya instead of hieroglyphics the surviving document carries a parallel translation into Spanish. Written in its current form immediately after the Spanish conquest, in about AD 1540, its authors probably had personal knowledge of the original text. Modern research has shown that the writers were probably a form of Maya priest called 'daykeepers'. It is even possible that the Mayan hieroglyphic original was their source, and that its being 'not seen' meant that it had been hidden from the Spanish.

As this book unfolds, we will discover that the Maya had very good reason to believe in the Great Cycles, the Suns, and especially the Prophecy. Good enough reason to base their entire culture on it; good enough reason to erect massive structures to fulfil it; and good enough reason to sacrifice hundreds if not thousands of human beings on account of it.

So, was this a local aberration of a primitive and bloodthirsty people? As we will see, it was far from a local belief; indeed, it almost certainly arrived from across the Atlantic. And those who brought it had every reason to take it seriously too.

As do we.

EXERCISE: PYRAMID VISUALISATIONS

The pyramid is a powerful Maya image. Maya pyramids combined the functions of tomb and temple, frequently containing the tomb of great leaders of the cities where they were built. Because the Maya believed, as did the Egyptians, that the dead had an influence on the living, a great ruler thus interred was able to influence later generations of rulers. The temple portion was on top of the pyramid, rather than inside it. Outside there was a stairway up the pyramid to the temple on top.

For the Maya as for the Egyptians, pyramids combine the symbolism of the Mother Mountain, with the primordial womb of their inner sanctuaries. As an archetypal symbol for use in visualisation, they are unsurpassed for tapping into ancient Maya wisdom. Several visualisations in this book will use pyramids and follow the same general format. The human mind works most powerfully in symbols, and by creating appropriate symbols our subconscious mind grasps their messages quickly, and begins to make the perceptual shifts necessary for our further personal growth.

This meditation uses the inner sanctum of the pyramid as a metaphor for the deep inner self, where all change begins.

☆ To start, close your eyes and visualise yourself standing at the head of a processional way, leading to the steps of a pyramid. It is night, the Time of the Gods, and the processional way is lit by blazing torches. You are dressed in initiation robes, and accompanied by softly chanting priests and a group of flute-players and drummers. It is a time of initiation, of going inward, to speak to the deepest level of your own being and to create intentions for your growth and expansion as a fully realised Being.

☆ The moment has come to start your journey. As you walk toward the pyramid, you are aware of the soft, warm, night breeze. With the exception of the soft chanting and muffled drumming, mixed with the muted tones of the flutes, there is utter stillness.

☆ As you reach the stairway going up the pyramid, the chanting stops and you proceed alone. The sacred chamber at the top of the pyramid is illuminated with torches. As you enter the cool stone surrounds you. As you walk further inward, you reach the doorway to the inner sanctum, and go inside.

☆ The inner sanctum is lit by a single torch, and waiting for you is the High Priest or Priestess, dressed in a robe of quetzal feathers. You are wordlessly directed to the stone bench in the exact centre of the chamber, where you sit. The air is full of the fragrance of copal-resin incense.

☆ Echoing around the chamber, are the simple words: 'May you find what you seek.' Then the Priest or Priestess exits silently, leaving you alone.

☆ As you sit quietly, begin to sense the expanse of the pyramid below and around you, and then the jungle beyond it. It becomes a real physical sensation, as if you yourself have expanded and are more connected to all that surrounds you. Through this connection, life itself is able to know and respond to our deepest needs. Remember that life responds to real needs, and not necessarily to our conscious wishes and desires. Let your intention in this moment of deeper connection be that life fulfils your highest need for inner knowing of the universal truths that are the foundation of Maya belief – and the foundation of all true belief. Take all the time you need in this step.

☆ Recognise that the path to the truth is an unfoldment. Life will only provide you with whatever serves you best at the time. It may appear that nothing has happened in this visualisation, but don't worry – life never refuses a request for truth.

☆ When you feel a sense of completion with the process, take a few deep breaths, and become aware of your surroundings again. When you are ready, your eyes will come open naturally.

2

The Evidence: The Old World

The evidence for comet impacts on Earth, as suggested by the Prophecy, falls into two general categories. First, is the evidence that comet impacts have occurred since human culture developed, affecting the evolution of civilisations. Within this category are Old World records, legends, and stories, as well as archaeological evidence.

In the following chapter we investigate the second general category – evidence possessed and passed down by the Maya themselves of an impact or impacts directly influencing Mesoamerica and/or the Maya world. In this category is both archaeological and written evidence from within Mesoamerica itself, and further south in South America, which was also affected. Also in this chapter we examine how knowledge of Old World events found its way to the Olmecs and was ultimately passed to and preserved by the Maya. In particular, this included an accurate calendar and its accompanying mathematics, which gave the Maya a timescale for both recording past events and forecasting future ones – the Prophecy.

Cycles of Time

Underlying the entire belief system to which the Prophecy belongs, is the notion of cycles of time. They are ultimately based on astronomical observation: the repeating positions of stars in the sky at certain times and the movement of planets. It is likely that some of the cycles are the direct result of periodic comet or meteor impacts.

The longest cycles were called Suns. Along with other Mesoamerican people – and people elsewhere – the Maya believe there have been four of them, and that we are now in the Fifth. The *Popol Vuh* describes them as follows:

☆ The First Sun, *Matlactli Atl:* duration 4,008 years. Those who lived then ate maize cold – *atzitziantli*.

☆ The Second Sun, *Ehecoatl:* duration 4,010 years. Those who lived then ate wild fruit known as *acotzintli*.

☆ The Third Sun, *Tleyquiyahuillo:* duration 4,081 years. Men, the descendants of the couple who were saved from the Second Sun ate a fruit called *tzincoacoc*.

☆ The Fourth Sun, *Tzontlilic:* duration 5,026 years. Men died of starvation after a deluge of flood and fire. . .

Descriptions of the ending of the four Suns correspond perfectly with the effects of known comet impacts.

Other 'Suns'

The idea of long-term cycles such as the 'Suns' is far from unique to the Maya. Buddhist scriptures also speak of 'Suns', of which there are to be seven, each one doomed to come to

an end by water, fire or wind. It is believed that we are
currently in the Seventh Sun, at the end of which 'the Earth
will break into flames'.

The Hopi Indians of Arizona, who may well derive their
traditions from the Aztecs, also talk about a series of world-
destroying cycles. Roy Willis's *World Mythology* describes
their foretelling of a coming catastrophic event:

> The first world was destroyed as a punishment for human
> misdemeanours, by an all consuming fire that came from
> above and below. The second world ended when the
> terrestrial globe toppled from its axis and everything was
> covered with ice. The third world ended in a universal
> flood. The present world is the fourth. Its fate will
> depend on whether or not its inhabitants behave in accor-
> dance with the Creator's plans.

In China we find a belief that Earth has gone through cyclic
destructions: each of the perished ages are called *Kis*, ten of
which are said to have elapsed up until the time of Confucius.
At the end of each *Kis*, in a great convulsion of nature, the sea
is carried out of its bed, mountains spring up out of the
ground, rivers change course, human beings are destroyed
and everything is ruined, and the ancient traces effaced.

Even in the Bible, II Peter 3 reminds us:

> We must be careful to remember that during the last days
> there are bound to be people who will be scornful and
> (who will say), everything goes on as it has since it began
> at the creation. They are choosing to forget that there
> were heavens at the beginning and that the earth was
> formed by the word of god out of water and between the
> waters, so that the world of that time was destroyed by

being flooded by water. By the same word, the present sky and earth are destined for fire . . . the Day of the Lord will come as a thief in the night, and then with a war the sky will vanish, the elements will catch fire and fall apart, and the earth and all it contains will be burned up.

Perhaps even more importantly, the belief in cycles of time is far from limited to ancient or extinct religions. One third or more of the world's living population belongs to religions based on it. It forms the entire foundation of Hinduism, which, on the broadest scale of things, has the Day of Brahma, a cyclic timespan spreading over millions of years. During a Brahma Day the universe expands and then contracts again, to be reborn in another expansion. Brahma, the creator, is but one dimension of the great god Vishnu; in his other aspects he remains himself, as the preserver of all, and in his other dimension he is Shiva, the destroyer. Thus this trinity recognises that all that is created is ultimately destroyed, and yet at the same time even in its destruction retains within it the seeds of its own rebirth. As ancient as this belief may be, it holds within it a reflection of modern science and its knowledge of the universe, which it is believed was born from a single ball of energy no larger than a pea, and is currently in a constant state of expansion until it reaches its final limits. Those limits and whether the universe will collapse in upon itself to be reborn in yet another cosmic explosion, another Big Bang, form the great questions of modern astrophysics. Perhaps the Hindus already have the answer.

On a smaller timescale, Hindus believe that we are living in the age called Kali Yuga, the last and most chaotic age of mankind. According to Indian astrologers, the Kali Yuga began in 3100 BC, a date corresponding almost exactly to that of the beginning of the Maya Long Count calendar.

The Maya Sky

Even a cursory examination of Maya culture reveals that it was fixated with the sky. Its major buildings were oriented to celestial features, its mathematics was specifically geared to the accurate compilation of tables for the movements of the moon and several planets, and the daily lives of the people were governed by the resulting astrology.

Starting at about the same time, almost all ancient cultures were doing the same. Beginning at roughly 2500 BC, there was a general shift from Earth Goddess religions, which saw Earth and nature itself as the governing deity of man, to the view of the deity as a male entity living in the sky, wrathful and meting out terrible justice to those who upset him. This is also the time when serious astronomical observations began to be made across much of the world. The Sumerians, Egyptians, Babylonians, Chinese, and the builders of Stonehenge, all started to make intense and accurate surveys of the sky, and entire civilisations began to be based on astrology – the omens and portents supposedly displayed in the sky. Why this sudden and intense interest in the sky?

Comets, Asteroids and Meteorites

Throughout history comets have been seen by most cultures as omens of doom. This has generally been dismissed as superstition, but there is growing evidence that the impact of both comet fragments and asteroids has been a much larger influence on the development and/or the decline of human civilisations than previously thought. Comets are no longer regarded as 'dirty snowballs', but as large accumulations of rock and other solid matter with the capacity to fragment and shower the planet with pieces — meteorites. That the dinosaurs were wiped out by the impact of a huge asteroid, a large stone or metal fragment of a planet that broke up between Mars and Jupiter is now no longer in doubt, but the effect of such impacts on human civilisation has largely been ignored until very recently.

Dr Bill Napier, astronomer at Armagh Observatory, believes that around the year 2350 BC, a large comet broke up near Earth, and the impact of some of its fragments ultimately brought to an end several ancient civilisations. Within a relatively few years of 2350 BC, the Old Kingdom of ancient Egypt, the Sumerian civilisation in Mesopotamia and the Harrapin culture of the Indus Valley in India all severely declined and collapsed.

Studies of tree rings from around the world have revealed that the planet suddenly cooled between 2354 and 2345 BC. Archaeologists excavating in northern Syria have discovered that a catastrophic event at that time caused the mud brick buildings of that area to disintegrate. Other researchers in the Middle East have found layers from around 2200 BC containing traces of minerals found only in meteorites. Further evidence suggests that much earlier impacts brought to an end the last Ice Age, as well as other dramatic climatic changes.

Dr Napier believes that the comet, named Encke, was responsible for the 2350 BC catastrophe, or, more correctly, a larger comet that broke up and of which Encke was a fragment. Other fragments of the same comet are encountered twice a year as the Earth passes through its tail of debris, creating the meteor shower called the Taurids. This may or may not be the same object that brought to an end each of the Maya Suns.

References to fires from the sky appear in most cultures, myths and religions. Many involve winged serpents battling in the heavens before one crashes to Earth. The Feathered Serpent widespread throughout Mesoamerica may be just such a 'creature'. The Book of Revelation describes a huge burning mountain falling from the sky, dropping hail and fire on Earth while the sun and moon are darkened. In the Old Testament Sodom and Gomorrah were destroyed by rain of fire and brimstone from the skies, while fireballs in the sky appear frequently in Babylonian astrology. The Book of Exodus records: 'There was hail and fire mingled with hail ... there was none like it in all the land of Egypt since it became a nation ... and the hail smote every herb of the field, and broke every tree of the field.' This may record the same event that destroyed Sodom and Gomorrah.

Flood Stories

There are two principal reasons to associate flood stories with comet impacts. Firstly, three-quarters of the Earth's surface is covered with water, so the odds are that a comet impact would occur in one of the oceans. A major impact could easily send 1,000-foot tidal waves hundreds of miles inland in low-lying regions. Secondly, an ocean impact would hurl many cubic miles of water into the atmosphere, with 'forty days and forty nights' of rain a real possibility. Even an impact on land would throw huge amounts of dust into the atmosphere, shifting weather patterns for years and increasing rainfall through an escalation in precipitation nucleii (the dust particles around which raindrops form and which are the basis of 'cloud seeding' to increase rainfall). We know that rainfall and weather patterns change dramatically for at least two years following a major volcanic eruption, which throws enormous amounts of dust high into the atmosphere. These would be mere shadows of a major impact.

Flood stories lie at the heart of virtually every ancient story and belief about the cycles of time, and provide evidence for comet impacts. The great scholar of mythology, the late Joseph Campbell, discovered similar flood stories in over 100 different cultures scattered across the whole of the earth. In India, a flood story is connected to the beginning of the Kali Yuga. Manu Satyavrata was warned by the god Vishnu of a forthcoming flood that would destroy the whole of mankind, and he built a giant ship loaded with two of every living species and the seeds of every plant. When the waters rose, Manu and his ark floated for many days and nights, finally coming to rest on a mountain top.

In the ancient writings of Mesopotamia, the most famous story is the epic of Gilgamesh, a king of ancient Sumeria. His story has been found in writings as early as the 3rd millennium BC. Gilgamesh experiences a number of heroic adventures, in his travels discovering the story of King Utnapishtim, who supposedly ruled thousands of years before Gilgamesh himself. This king had a story much like the story of Noah. The god Ea spoke to him, and warned him of an impending catastrophe, which was about to occur because the misdeeds of humankind offended the gods. He was told to tear down his house and build a boat, and put aboard it the seed of all living things. Soon a great catastrophe flooded the face of the Earth. After a period of time the waters receded and the king and his retinue ascended from the boat to re-establish life upon the barren Earth.

Evidence of Floods and Impacts

But what is the physical evidence of a great flood? Excavations across much of Mesopotamia have uncovered a layer of barren mud, varying from a few centimetres to several metres in thickness, deeply buried in the many-layered ruins of ancient cities. In most instances there was evidence of habitation below the mud, but in every location the habitation was of a very different nature from that found above. There clearly had been a long break between the periods in which the areas were inhabited.

Since 1980 interest has grown in locating and dating recent impact craters on Earth. In the 1960s only a small handful of craters were known or even acknowledged by geologists, but hundreds have now been discovered. Studies of the near-space environment have started to reveal a great many objects in orbits that cross Earth's orbit. All are potential impacts. In 1989 an asteroid named 4581 Asclepius missed collision with Earth by only six hours. Approximately 0.5 kilometres in diameter, it would have released energy equivalent to more than 1,000 one-megaton bombs. Had it impacted, history would have taken an abrupt turn in 1989! Yet this was not the closest passage: in 1937 the asteroid Hermes, with a diameter of 1.2 kilometres, passed even closer.

Several major astronomers believe that about 50,000 years ago a giant comet settled into an Earth-crossing orbit. About 20,000 years ago it began to fragment. About 17,000 years ago large fragments of this comet started to impact on Earth, causing climatic changes dramatic enough to end the last Ice Age. And subsequent strikes by fragments of the comet have had a dramatic impact on civilisations throughout the world. When we examine the time periods ascribed to the first Four Suns of the Maya we see a very close general correlation in their lengths, especially given the difficulty in maintaining an accurate record following such events, much less four of them. It is not difficult to imagine a large, fragmenting comet in a long-term orbit, with some of its fragments impacting with the Earth every 5,000 years or so.

The Maya prediction for 'the end of the world' in the year 2012 may in fact have a sound scientific basis. The table below sums up the related time correlations:

First Sun	Began 15,213 BC	A close correlation with the beginning of the end of the last Ice Age and the dates given to frozen mammoths.
Second Sun	Began 11,205 BC	A good correlation with the end of the last Ice Age, and the drying up of the Sahara, leading to Egyptian civilisation developing along the Nile. Most accounts place the end of Atlantis at this time.
Third Sun	Began 8000 BC	A likely correlation with Mesopotamian flood deposits and Gilgamesh and Noah stories.
Fourth Sun	Began 3114 BC	An excellent correlation with the founding of Egyptian and Sumerian high civilisations and the beginning of Kali Yuga in India. A likely correlation with Tiahuanaco events (see Chapter 3).

Not only the Maya or the Mesopotamians have possible records of impact events. Some histories record the actual meteorites themselves. There is reference in Jewish legend to a sacred stone that might be a meteorite: the Eben Shetiyah. This was referred to as the Foundation Stone, upon which the Temple at the heart of Jerusalem was built. Also, according to Jewish legend, this was the stone pillow used by Jacob when he had his famous dream of angels ascending and descending a ladder to heaven. It is suggested in both the Book of Chronicles and the Book of Samuel that a 'fire from heaven' struck the altar in Jerusalem.

In Greece, the famous Omphaloas Stone of Delphi was believed to have fallen from heaven. In Greek mythology the stone was said to have been the one fed in place of the infant Zeus to the time god Cronus, who devoured his own children. After Zeus grew to manhood, he drove Cronus from the sky and into the very depths of the universe. First though, he was forced to vomit up the stone, which landed in the exact 'centre of the world' – in the shrine at Delphi.

In Egypt, the most venerated object in the Old Kingdom, which began about 3100 BC, was the *Ben-ben*. It rested atop a pedestal in its own temple in Heliopolis, north of modern Cairo, the centre of Egyptian religion at that time. Egyptologists have long speculated that the Ben-ben was a meteorite, and even that it had a pyramidal shape, suggesting to the Egyptians that the shape had divine significance. It was said to be made from *bja* metal, meaning 'metal from heaven'. It is possible that the entire spate of pyramid-building in Egypt sprang from the fall of this one object, which fell some centuries previous to the 2350 BC fall that brought the Old Kingdom to an end. Indeed, it may have been part of a meteor shower that occurred before 3200 BC, which ended whatever civilisation the Egyptians and Sumerians – and perhaps even the Olmecs – inherited their culture from.

Further north, in Arabia, it is possible and even likely that the Kaaba stone, venerated by Muslims and one of the objects of the annual pilgrimage to Mecca, is a meteorite. There is also evidence that a meteorite may once have been worshipped in the ancient Andes. One of the titles the Incas gave to Viracocha was Illa-Tika. This is translated as 'original thunderstone', which sounds very much like a meteorite.

On a longer timescale, one of the great mysteries of geology has been the frozen mammoths discovered in Siberia and Alaska. Inevitably these animals are found in a partially dismembered state, along with the shattered remains of trees and other plant life. It seems as if some gigantic force had smashed into them and hurled them in heaps. F. C. Hibben of the University of Mexico says:

> Although the formation of deposits of silt, muck and bones is not clear there is ample evidence that at least portions of this material were deposited under catastrophic conditions. Mammalian remains are for the most part dismembered and disarticulated . . . Twisted and torn trees are piled into splintered masses.

This is precisely what one would expect from the gigantic tidal waves generated by an ocean impact. What has puzzled scientists studying these remains is that frequently the mammoths are found with undigested meals still in their stomachs, as if they were in the process of eating at the very moment of death. In addition, the flowers and plants present in their stomachs indicate that they died in the summer, during warm weather. How then, did they become quick-frozen? We now know that an impact-generated tidal wave could easily have carried debris hundreds of miles inland. The possibility must surely exist that, if this is what happened to the mammoths, their remains were moved to a location where the weather was still freezing cold. The relatively instantaneous drop in temperature because of atmospheric debris could also have contributed to the process. As in the case of the remains at Tiahuanaco, in Peru, which we will explore later.

Thus we discover that there is indeed strong evidence of comet or meteor impacts that have influenced the course of human history, and that there was Old World knowledge that could have been passed on to the Olmecs and eventually the Maya.

But the Maya had information of their own which, when added to the Old World knowledge, put them in a unique position.

3

The Evidence: The New World

Did the Maya also record any events in their history that might record the effects of comet impacts? Full descriptions of the end of each of the 'Suns', feature in the *Popol Vuh* (see over).

Other Catastrophes Recorded in the Popol Vuh

Aside from the events that ended each Sun, the *Popol Vuh* also records a vivid description of another major catastrophe. It is unclear whether it refers to events at the end of the last Sun, or whether it records another one, but the descriptions are entirely consistent with an impact event:

They were pounded down to the bones and tendons, smashed and pulverised, even to the bones. The earth was blackened because of this; the black rainstorm began, rain all day and rain all night.

The stones, their hearth stones were shooting out, coming right out of the fire.

First Sun	Matlactli Atl	Duration 4,008 years	The First Sun was destroyed by water in the sign matlactli atl [ten water]. It was called apachiohualiztli [flood, deluge]... Some say that only one couple escaped, protected by an old tree living near the water. Others say that there were seven couples who hid in a cave until the flood was over and the waters had gone down. They re-populated the earth and were worshipped as gods in their nations ...
Second Sun	Ehecoatl	Duration 4,010 years	This Sun was destroyed by ehecoatl [wind serpent] ... one man and one woman, standing on a rock, were saved from destruction ...
Third Sun	Tleyquiyahuillo	Duration 4,081 years	This Sun was destroyed by fire...
Fourth Sun	Tzontlilic	Duration 5,026 years	Men died of starvation after a deluge of flood and fire...

They want to climb up on the houses, but they fall as the houses collapse.

They want to climb the trees; they're thrown off by the trees.

They want to get inside caves, but the caves slam shut in their faces.

The sky-earth was already there, but the face of the sun-moon was clouded over. There came a rain of resin from the sky.

During this catastrophe, certain of the 'gods' appeared and attacked the few survivors of the catastrophe:

There came the one named Gouger of Faces: he gouged out their eyeballs.

There came Sudden Bloodletter: he snapped off their heads.

There came Crunching Jaguar: he ate their flesh.

There came Tearing Jaguar: he tore them open.

The Maya gods are metaphors for the forces of nature, so we see that other natural disasters followed the initial catastrophe. It is unknown exactly which forces are described in these metaphors, but the first list of calamities is highly credible as a record of an impact event: the violent shaking from the impact itself, the hearthstones shooting out and the collapse of houses; the rain of fire and resin, from petroleum byproducts released by the heat of the impact; the darkening of the sun and moon, from impact debris; the fall of hail from moisture hurled high into the atmosphere to freeze before falling back; and the subsequent cooling of the region, from effects similar to a 'nuclear winter'.

The *Popol Vuh* recounts a time when the Maya (or at least

some antecedent of the Maya) experienced a period of intense cold – in tropical Yucatán: 'And so again the tribes arrived, again done in by the cold. Thick were the white hail, the blackening storm, and white crystals. The cold was incalculable. They were simply overwhelmed.'

Yet another passage in the *Popol Vuh* appears to describe an impact event, possibly the same event referred to above: 'And when the sun had risen just a short distance he was like a person, and his heat was unbearable. Since he revealed himself *only when he was born*, it is only his reflection that now remains. As they put it in the ancient text, "the visible sun is not the real one."' This clearly reveals that recollections of impact-like events were written down in a text much older than the *Popol Vuh*. The just-born sun in the recollection sounds like an impact fireball, one whose 'heat was unbearable'.

The *Popol Vuh* also contains an account of how a number of the tribes of the Maya came to have different names for their gods and different languages. In one intriguing line, we read that, like their gods, their language was 'differentiated on account of a *stone* [a meteorite?] . . . when they came from Tulan in the darkness [after the impact?]. All the tribes were sown and came to light in unity, and each division was allocated a name for its god.'

Other Evidence from South America

In the Andes of South America there is another flood story similar in its content to both the Old World and the Maya flood stories. The god Tezcatilpoca brought a flood to destroy all mankind, sending a warning only to Tezpi, who floated away on a huge ship with his wife, children, a large number of animals and birds and supplies of grains and seeds. As the flood retreated, the vessel came to rest on a mountain top. Tezpi and his family then proceeded to replant and repopulate the earth.

And South America produces more than just written evidence. A startling discovery was made at Lake Titicaca, in Peru. The city of Tiahuanaco, on its shores, is one of the great mysteries of modern archaeology. Few archaeologists can agree on a date for its foundation, with estimates varying from 2000 BC or even earlier to the 9th century AD. One thing is certain: the building of the city had virtually nothing to do with the Incas, whose civilisation rose to the peak of its influence only a century before the Spanish conquest.

But Tiahuanaco contains an even greater mystery than the date of its establishment. As early as 1945, archaeologist Arthur Posansky proposed a very early date for a catastrophic event, suggesting that a combination of flood and earthquake produced the evidence he found: 'chaotic disorder among wrought stones, utensils, tools, and an endless variety of other things. All of this had been moved, broken, and accumulated in a confused heap.' Mixed among the debris were remains of humans as well as fish and shells from the lake, and 'layers of alluvium [water-laid sand and gravel] cover the whole field of ruins, and lacusterine [lake-originated] sand mixed with shells from Titicaca ... accumulated in places surrounded by walls'. A flood had certainly occurred, leaving deposits chillingly similar to those of the frozen mammoths. But what caused it, and why the evidence of its violence? Was it caused by an earthquake, or by the violent shaking of the ground by a nearby impact?

In Argentina, a chain of small impact craters dating from around 2900 BC has been discovered along an 18-kilometre track. Although this is over a thousand miles from Lake Titicaca, there is no reason to assume that craters have been found only for objects that fell at the same time. Other, larger objects may well have fallen further north, both near Lake Titicaca and in Yucatán. Equally, dating of impact events is an inexact science, and the date of the fall could easily be closer to 3100 BC. This could even have been part of a wider fall, some of which may have landed in the Old World.

There is further evidence that the Titicaca flood was caused by an impact. The climate in the region also underwent a serious change after the catastrophic event that destroyed the city. It became colder and archaeological evidence shows that the survivors, after a struggle to adapt and survive, eventually moved to better climes.

Ancient Connections

Now we begin to see the real significance of the Maya Prophecy, and the incredible gift to humanity of the Maya. Of all the civilisations of the Earth, the Maya have preserved in their records not only actual descriptions of an impact event, but even more significantly, *they have given us a timescale*, thanks to their dedication to their calendar and mathematics. Although Old World civilisations refer to and believe in cyclic time, none of them present us with such accurate records. It is likely that they existed in many other societies, but none have survived cultural disintegration and upheaval. Only one ancient civilization possessed an accurate calendar with which to time the events: Egypt.

It appears that there were two separate but connected occurrences: firstly, the comet/asteroid/meteorite impact recorded in the *Popol Vuh*, then, the arrival of the 'bearded white men', who brought the calendar and mathematics from the Old World along with recollections of the same or similar events that were passed to the Olmecs. Or it is possible that these men may have actually *been* the Olmecs.

'Bearded White Men'

There are a number of variations on the 'bearded white men' story, and it appears that a mixture of several stories has found its way to us across time. They are too widespread through the whole of the ancient Americas to dismiss. The Olmecs, Toltecs and Maya in Mesoamerica and the Incas in Peru had not only spoken and written legends but also ancient stone carvings clearly representing bearded Caucasians, long predating the coming of the Spanish. Indeed, the Spanish conquest of the Aztecs was directly aided by these legends: the arrival of Cortez and his men was believed to be the promised return of Quetzalcoatl and his followers.

Archaeologists have tended to dismiss these legends for a lack of 'evidence', ignoring the fact that the legends themselves are the evidence. Only a few generations of archaeologists ago the Bible, in particular the Old Testament, was similarly considered to be merely myth and legend, until biblical archaeology emerged around 1930. It has made many startling discoveries, each underlining the Old Testament as an accurate history of the times. It is a lesson Mesoamerican archaeologists need to remember.

It seems likely that the earliest Mesoamerican appearance of the mysterious Founder (or Founders) occurred in Olmec Mexico, the first culture to show any evidence of the effects of his appearance. Stories of the Founder passed down through the Toltecs to the Aztecs, who called him Quetzalcoatl, meaning 'Plumed Serpent'. Carvings in Olmec contexts clearly show bearded white men who, in fact, look exactly like the Phoenicians represented in profile in Mediterranean stone carvings. Are these necessarily the bearded white men of legend? It is impossible to be certain. There is no reason to suppose that if Mediterranean, African, or Oriental peoples reached Mesoamerica, they did so only once. Not a single artefact has ever been found to demonstrate an origin outside Mesoamercia, so it must equally be assumed that there was no flourishing trade with the outside world.

Let us now briefly examine some of the bearded white men stories, because whoever they were, it is almost certain that they brought the timing of the Prophecy with them.

Quetzalcoatl

Early stories of Quetzalcoatl, collected in Mexico by Spanish chroniclers, described him as 'a fair and ruddy-complexioned man with a long beard' and as 'a white man; a large man, broad browed, with huge eyes, long hair, and a great, rounded beard'. It is also said of him that he 'condemned sacrifices, except of fruits and flowers, and was known as the god of peace . . . when addressed on the subject of war he is reported to have stopped up his ears with his fingers'. Another widely known tradition of Quetzalcoatl is that he 'came from across the sea in a boat that moved by itself without paddles. He built houses and showed couples that they could live together as husband and wife; and since people often quarrelled in those days, he taught them to live in peace.'

Quetzalcoatl's symbol was the snake. One is led to wonder whether this is the Egyptian cobra, symbol of the Egyptian royal house; its spread hood might have appeared as a 'plume'. Ancient Maya religious texts known as the Books of Chilam Balam report that the first inhabitants of Yucatán were the 'people of the serpent', who came from the east in boats, with their leader, whose name meant 'serpent of the east'. He was reputed to be a healer who could cure by laying on hands and also revived the dead. In many respects this resembles a description of the Egyptian god Horus, who was, among other things, the god of healing.

Kukulcán (meaning 'Feathered Serpent' in Mayan) was the Maya counterpart of the Aztec/Toltec/Olmec Quetzalcoatl. In the Maya pantheon he was regarded as the great organiser, founder of cities, the maker of laws and the teacher of the calendar. His attributes and life history are so human that it is not improbable that he may have been a real historical character, some great law-giver and organiser, whose bene-factions lingered after death and whose personality was eventually deified.

The stories of the Maya Kukulcán and the Toltec Quetzalcoatl are nearly identical. The name 'Kukulcán' appeared in the Maya pantheon only at the time of the conquest of Chichén by the exiled Toltecs in AD 983. It is likely that it was incorporated into Maya belief at that time, as he does not appear beforehand, as far as can be deter-mined. But another 'god', Itzamná who appeared much earlier has a story not dissimilar to Kukulcán's and is possibly the original 'Kukulcán'.

The oldest god of the Maya Olympus, Itzamná has many of the characteristics of Quetzalcoatl. He is always represented as a wizened old man. It is entirely possible that he is Quetzalcoatl in early Maya form. According to some Maya texts perhaps as many as 20 men came from the east in boats and stayed for ten years. Their leader was Itzamná, meaning 'Serpent of the East', a healer who used the laying on of hands and revived the dead. The companions were described as wearing flowing robes and sandals, and they had long beards and bare heads. These traditions describe some as 'gods of fish', 'gods of agriculture' and a 'god of thunder', 'gods' probably meaning 'teachers'. The father of mathemat-ics, metallurgy and astronomy, Kukulcán/Itzamná was believed to have introduced the knowledge of writing into Central America, to have brought the calendar, and to have been a master builder. He was also a teacher who taught that no living thing was to be harmed, and that sacrifices were to be made not of human beings, but of birds and butterflies. Were Quetzalcoatl/Kukulcán/Itzamná the same historical figure, or did several teachers arrive at different places in Mesoamerica? It seems most likely that they are one and the same.

The *Popol Vuh* records the legend of the great quest undertaken by intrepid Maya pilgrims to the centre of all Mesoamerican civilisation: Tula. Three nobles 'journeyed to the east' and 'passed over the sea' to 'receive lordship'. The lord of the east, whom the *Popol Vuh* names as Nacxit, was described as 'the great lord and sole judge over a populous domain'. During their stay with Nacxit they were given emblems of kingship and were apparently given education. They 'brought back the writing of Tulan, the writing of Zuyua [sounding similar to 'Libya', the ancient Egyptian name for 'Egypt'], and they spoke of their investiture in their signs and in their words'. When these nobles returned, they resumed their lordship over the tribes that they represented. It is also said that at the times of their deaths 'their faces did not die; they passed them on', a possible reference to Egyptian-style death masks, which appear in Maya entombments. Whether they in fact went to Egypt or to Olmec Tula, as seems more likely, the use of Egyptian-sounding names and Egyptian cultural symbols could easily have been part of the Olmec culture. For all we know, the Olmecs themselves may have been Egyptians, perhaps fleeing from the upheavals at the collapse of the Old Kingdom, when Egypt came under the yoke of the Hyskos.

Egyptian Clues

How did this evidence pointing to an Egyptian connection find its way to the Olmecs from the other side of the Atlantic? A strong clue is that the 'bearded white men' arrived in a 'boat made of snakes', a perfect description of a reed boat, with its undulations in the waves appearing as the writhing of snakes. 'Moving without paddles' is possible with a simple device that might not be immediately apparent to people who had not yet discovered it: a sail. Such boats were in use in civilisations around the Mediterranean and Nile long before 2000 BC, and well before the supposed founding of the Olmec culture.

Other evidence comes from similarities between the Egyptian calendar and the Olmec/Maya Solar Year calendar (referred to as the 'Vague Year'). Almost uniquely among ancient peoples, both possessed the knowledge that the Earth's year is a little over 365 days. While differing in the number of months, each have a basic 360-day period, plus five extra days. It was not until just a few centuries ago that we in the Western world had a calendar as accurate. How did two cultures an ocean apart gain such accuracy?

Not only that, the earliest archaeological evidence for the Olmec civilisation starts about 2000 BC, so, why did they use a calendar that begins in 3114 BC? In searching for the reason for the beginning of the Long Count calendar, archaeologists have thrashed about for an explanation. The best they have come up with is 'it must have been determined in later centuries by calculation backward into the time range of creation and mythical events'. Such is the political correctness of archaeology that no orthodox archaeologist has dared to suggest a connection to the foundation of the Egyptian and Sumerian civilisations. The current state of our knowledge gives us no final answer. Did the Egyptians bring it to

Mesoamerica? Very possibly. Did an even older culture bring it to both places? Also very possibly, although exactly where and what this culture may have been is impossible to determine at the moment. And if it was brought to Mesoamerica, whether by the Egyptians or someone else, did the Prophecy come along with it?

Almost certainly.

One significant indicator is an inscription at Palenque that places the 'births of the gods' at around the same time as the beginning of the current Great Cycle, the Fifth Sun. The identity of the 'gods' is not specified, but if it refers to the civilisers who arrived with the 'god' Quetzalcoatl, then their arrival occurs some time after 3114 BC, a date that falls within a few decades of the founding of both the Egyptian and Sumerian civilisations, which also seemed to appear from nowhere. A coincidence?

Other parallels with ancient Egypt and Mesopotamia are astonishing. Eminent Egyptologist Walter Emery, states:

> At a period approximately 3200 BC, a great change took place in Egypt, and the country passed rapidly from a state of [stone age] culture . . . to one of well-organised monarchy . . . writing appears, monumental architecture and the arts and crafts developed to an astonishing degree, and all the evidence points to the existence of a luxurious civilisation. All this was achieved within a comparative short period of time, for there appears to be little or no background to these fundamental developments in writing and architecture.

Just like the Olmecs.

At the same time, Sumer on the Lower Euphrates also began to flower without any apparent developmental phase.

There are many similarities to the Egyptian flowering, and it has even been suggested that Sumer may have been the model for the newly founded Egyptian civilisation. But Professor Emery writes:

> The impression we get is of an indirect connection, and perhaps the existence of a third party, whose influence spread to both the Euphrates and the Nile . . . a third party whose cultural achievements were passed on independently to Egypt and Mesopotamia would best explain the common features and fundamental differences between the two civilisations.

And, perhaps also, the Olmecs.

The Cloud People

This could have been dismissed as mere myth and speculation until recent discoveries in Peru cast a whole new light on the question of 'bearded white men'. Explorer Gene Savoy discovered extensive ruins in the high mountains of northern Peru, an area said by the Incas at the time of the Spanish conquest to be the home of the 'Cloud People'. According to the stories the Incas told to the Spanish chroniclers, they had only conquered the Cloud People in the 1480s, just a century before the arrival of the Spanish. They described them as 'beautiful people' – tall, blue-eyed, blond and white-skinned. They supposedly lived in seven great cities in the Chachapoyas area of the Andes.

While the Spanish dismissed the Inca claims, Gene Savoy wasn't so sure. Starting in the 1970s, he made several expeditions to the Chachapoyas area. In the vicinity of the Lake of the Condors, he made an exciting discovery: a huge, ancient city. Nearby were cliff tombs, unknown elsewhere in South

America, which contained the mummies of tall, white people embalmed in a way never before seen in South America, and similar to Egyptian mummies. The skin had been treated with an as yet unknown substance to prevent decay in the humid jungle and the internal organs had been removed.

Later expeditions to the area, this time with Peruvian archaeologists, revealed the existence of further cliff tombs, and a huge city covered by the jungle, now named Gran Valaya. Over 60 square miles, it is the largest intact archaeological site in the world. Nearby is the massive fortress called Quelap, with walls 60 feet high and a perimeter two-thirds of a mile long. It contains more stone than the Great Pyramid in Egypt.

Savoy speculates that it is entirely possible that boats from Egypt or Mesopotamia could have arrived from across the Atlantic and sailed up the Amazon to within relatively easy distance of Chachapoyas. This idea was recently explored by the BBC television programme *QED* in 'Secrets of the Cloud People'. So, were these Cloud People connected to the legends of Quetzalcoatl/Kukulcán/Itzamná further north in Mexico and Yucatán? Are they connected in some way to Viracocha, the Peruvian equivalent of Quetzalcoatl? Whoever the Cloud People turn out to be, it adds to the body of evidence of contact with Old World civilisations.

Mythological Similarities

Further evidence of an Olmec/Maya–Egyptian connection lies in the distinct similarity of the essential mythology of both the Maya and the Egyptians. In ancient times it was the fashion to cast spiritual revelations in stories of mythology. Myths contain truths about human life in terms that go beyond expression in cold facts and figures or rational thought. Myths deal in archetypes, biologically grounded, elementary ideas presented in the form of metaphors.

We can be certain that when the metaphors – which are different for each culture – are similar, then the fundamental understandings of life and the universe will be as well. This is the case with the Egyptians and the Olmec/Maya. Both mythologies demonstrate a mutual understanding of the essential duality of life: up/down, hot/cold, good/evil, life/death, underworld/overworld.

In Egyptian mythology, Isis and her husband Osiris were twins, born from the goddess Nut, Mother Nature. Their younger brother and sister, Seth and Nephtys, were also twins, born likewise from Nut. One night Osiris mistakenly made love to Nephtys, thinking she was Isis, and from that mistaken union, was born Osiris's oldest son, Anubis. Nephtys's twin, Seth, displeased with this event, killed Osiris, his older brother. Osiris's sarcophagus floated down the Nile, to be washed up on a beach in faraway Syria (an Egyptian metaphor for the 'back end of nowhere', and the equivalent of the Maya underworld). Isis took on human form and went to Syria to retrieve Osiris's body. She had relations with Osiris's corpse, and conceived Horus – 'out of death comes life'. Osiris became a resurrection figure in Egyptian mythology. The annual rebirth and resurrection of the Nile – that is, the annual inundation of the Nile – is said to be connected to the resurrection of Osiris.

In Maya mythology, after three unsuccessful attempts to create humanity, during the first three Suns, the gods sought the counsel of Xpiyacoc, a divine matchmaker, and Xmucane, a divine midwife. From them were born twin sons, One-Hunahpu and Seven-Hunahpu, and together with the daughter of the Lord of the Underworld, Blood Gatherer, they in turn gave birth to twin sons, jointly fathered. The sons are Hunahpu and Xbalanque, who embarked on a series of adventures in the underworld, an archetypal hero quest like that of Isis. One-Hunahpu and Seven-Hunahpu also experienced trials and initiations in the underworld, culminating with the overthrow of the Lords of Xilbalbá, the Lords of the Underworld. Death and resurrection play a major part in their story, and they became resurrection figures, like Osiris and Horus.

Similarities in mythologies do not necessarily prove a direct link, though on the other hand they do suggest a common source.

Other Possible Contacts

Further evidence says that white men were not the only people to cross the Atlantic. The most mysterious of all of the Olmec carvings are giant heads with negroid features. Over 30 of these heads have been found, many of them up to 8 feet in diameter and weighing many tons. Carved deliberately and precisely in black basalt, a hard, dense volcanic stone, they have been discovered at San Lorenzo and other locations in Yucatán and Guatemala. Again, one may speculate on their origins.

Other highly developed ancient cultures had evolved in Africa aside from Egypt: Zimbabwe was a major and flourishing civilisation several thousand years ago; other extensive and well-developed black civilisations like the Kushites left their evidence throughout much of Africa. Nubia, Egypt's southern neighbour and sometime province, would have shared many of the Egyptians' sailing and navigational skills. The possibility of black people's contact with Mesoamerica certainly exists.

But the Mediterranean and African peoples are not the only possible source of the Olmec/Maya civilisation. The 260-day Sacred Calendar, with its 20 named-days as a sequence of animals, is similar to the lunar zodiacs of many Oriental and Southeast Asian civilisations. Common ground is also found in the Olmec/Maya cosmology of four sacred cardinal directions, each with an associated colour, plant, animal and god. The Olmec/Maya saw a rabbit in the face of the full moon, as did the Asians. Even more significant, perhaps, is that astronomers in the Han Dynasty of China used exactly the same calculations to predict solar and lunar eclipses. The ancient Orientals were advanced sailors and navigators, and Chinese manuscripts dating to about 500 BC describe journeys along the coastline of a faraway land that some historians suggest matches the west coast of North America and Mexico. Dr Paul Tolstoy, who made a detailed study of the tools and preparation of bark paper around the Pacific basin, clearly believes that similar techniques to those used by the Maya and Aztecs were spread around the Pacific from Indonesia to Mesoamerica.

In summary, we have two separate but connected events, first, the comet/asteroid/meteorite impact recorded in the *Popol Vuh*, then the arrival with the 'bearded white men' of the calendar and mathematics from the Old World, along with Old World recollections of the same or similar impact events. Whether these earliest teachers were Egyptians or from some civilisation that predated both the Egyptians and the Olmecs is impossible to say for certain. If it is an even earlier civilisation, we can find little evidence of it. But there are stories. The Greeks preserved the story of Atlantis, an island that was destroyed in a great cataclysm. So do the Maya.

An Older Culture Destroyed?

In the Madrid Codex, there is a description of the lost Island of 'Mu', a land where terrible earthquakes occurred, the land torn asunder and sinking into the sea with its millions of inhabitants. The Codex gives no name to this island, so the name 'Mu' was coined by an Englishman, James Churchward, believing it to be the place inhabited by the Lemurians, as described in his book *The Lost Continent of Mu* (1930). In fact the entire 'esoteric' tradition of Mu, now widely discussed in New Age circles, comes entirely from this single reference in the Codex. The story sounds like that of Atlantis.

With the Maya recollection of a terrible catastrophe, the availability of a calendar must have seemed like a blessing beyond imagination. Is it then any wonder that the Maya took the calendar and mathematics so seriously? Because celestial events were attributed to the gods, is it likewise any wonder that they were willing to devote huge portions of their culture to building temples and observatories and even to attempt to placate the gods with blood? For them, it was a matter of life and death itself.

It is very likely to mean the same for us, too. In the following chapters we will examine the Maya in more detail, to emphasise why we should take the Prophecy as seriously as they did.

4

Maya Astronomy

Such was the Maya obsession with the sky that they replicated it at every opportunity. Most major buildings in virtually every Maya city show not only astronomical alignments in their construction, but that they were also used for astronomical observations and calculations. Doorways and windows were positioned so that the movements of planets and other celestial objects could be observed and measured. At Uxmal, all buildings are aligned in the same direction, except for one. Within that building, an observer looking out through the central doorway towards a mound 3.5 miles away would see Venus rise just above that mound when it rises at its southernmost extreme. At the Caracol at Chichén Itzá, the entire building is aligned to the northerly extremes of Venus, with another window creating a diagonal sightline with the planet's setting position at its southernmost location.

For the Maya, the one particular indicator of dark happenings was the rising or setting of Venus. Virtually unique among the astronomers of the ancient world, the Maya knew that the Morning and Evening Stars were the same object and made extensive and highly accurate studies of the movement of Venus. Tables devoted to the subject form considerable portions of the surviving Codices. In the Maya world-view Venus played a similar role to that of Mars in the Old World, as a symbol of war. In inscriptions, a Venus glyph is often found placed above another glyph, often that of a city attacked. The date selected for the attack was usually determined by astrology, and particularly by the position of Venus.

In an example well-documented in Maya inscriptions, the first visibility of Venus as the Evening Star in December AD 735 was the signal for an attack of the town of Siebal by the nearby town of Dos Pilas, leading to the capture of its ruler. The highest goal in warfare for the Maya was to capture the ruler of another city-state in battle, and to torture and humiliate him, often for years, at the end of which he would become an offering to the gods, usually by decapitation. Presumably this was the highest offering the winners' city could make, and certain favours could be expected of the gods in return. The ruler of Siebal was kept alive for 12 years in order to be sacrificed at a particular conjunction of Venus.

This case points out one of the main causes of warfare among the city-states of the Maya: the need for captives for ritual sacrifice. That such attacks were often triggered by celestial events again underlines the need for human sacrifice among the Maya at particularly 'hazardous' astronomical moments. Why were particular astronomical conditions seen as so dangerous that they needed the offering of human life to prevent some dreadful occurrence? Why were certain conditions in particular considered so hazardous that they required a city to go to war with another, specifically to capture its ruler as a high-status offering? As, indeed, was the belief regarding certain astronomical conditions in many other parts of the ancient world.

The answer must lie with some dreadful celestial event in the past, at a time when Venus was prominent to the Maya. Its effects affected many civilisations worldwide, and were catastrophic enough that those civilisations would undertake virtually anything – such as human and animal sacrifice and the building of gigantic structures to placate the gods – in order to prevent its recurrence. Few celestial happenings could strike such terror into the hearts of men, but an impact of a comet fragment or fragments is certainly one of them.

Mars also was an important symbol to the Maya, although its exact interpretation astrologically is uncertain. It was studied almost as much as Venus, and accurate tables of the position of Mars, based on repetitions of the number 78 (Mars has a year of 780 days) are present in the Dresden Codex. There also appear to be symbolic and ritual associations with Jupiter, for both its full solar year of 12 Earth years and its half-cycle.

The Sky

The Maya believed the universe to be a three-part structure: the Overworld, the Middleworld and the Underworld. The Overworld was the day sky, illuminated by the sun; the Underworld was the night sky, which passed over humanity daily. The world was believed to be flat; the heavens rotated around it, with both the Overworld and the Underworld making an appearance once every 24-hour cycle. The flat Earth was believed to rest on the back of a monstrous crocodile, relaxing in a pool of waterlilies. Its counterpart in the sky was a double-headed serpent, expressed by the Milky Way, which was believed to be the mystic road that one travelled after death on one's passage into the Underworld. In representations of the sky serpent, we see attached to it symbols for the sun, moon, Venus and other astronomical bodies.

The Middleworld was the world of humans, divided into four quarters determined by the cardinal points of the compass, each direction designated by a tree, a bird and a colour. Thus the days of the Ritual Almanac calendar moved through coloured space in a counter-clockwise direction. The three levels were joined with a central tree, with its roots plunging into the Underworld and its branches reaching up into the Overworld. This central tree was green, with four further trees each at a cardinal direction and each having its own colour. The red tree signified the east and the rising sun; the white tree, the north, and the ancestral dead; the yellow, the south, and the right hand of the sun; and the black, the west and the Underworld.

The Overworld heavens were arranged in 13 layers, with specific deities and celestial bodies assigned to each of them, although they were in continuous interaction rather than separate from each other. The Underworld had nine such levels, each also with its own god.

Cities and Temples

By the time of the first beginnings of building in the Maya world, further north in Mexico the Toltecs and Olmecs had long before erected massive pyramids, temples and palaces. It is from their influence that Maya monumental architecture really took hold.

The drawing together of the many threads of Maya culture to create the great cities of the Classic period first took shape in the southern lowlands, in the Tikal–Uaxactún region. There is no evidence of a great population increase in either location but the erection of public buildings accelerated dramatically. This may indicate when Maya religion became more formalised and began to make greater demands on the culture. It may also correspond with the arrival of the Prophecy from the Olmecs, and with it the need to erect huge buildings to keep the gods happy and serve as observatories to plot accurately the movements of the heavens. It is perhaps not unlike the growing position of the Catholic Church in Europe during the Middle Ages, when it increasingly came to dominate daily life. The great cathedrals of Europe began to rise during this time, again in a situation perhaps not dissimilar to that of the Maya, or the Egyptians and Sumerians a millennium before.

At the end of every 52-year Calendar Round cycle (page 97), a new layer of construction was added to the outside of existing temples and monuments, creating difficulty in determining exactly the point at which Maya cities began to coalesce and develop monumental architecture. Where collapse and erosion have exposed the internal portions of pyramids and temples, building after building has been discovered, rather like the layers of a Russian doll. The oldest are usually buried deep in the centre. We know that several centuries before the birth of Christ, significant cities were established at a number of places, including Tikal, Copán and Palenque. Temples were the largest and most prominent buildings, but palaces and other high-status structures were also built.

This time also marked the widening of the gap between people of high status and those of low. The dwellings and burial places of aristocrats – from which group the Maya priesthood were drawn – were impressive stone structures, in contrast to the daub and wattle construction of the typical peasant house. A very small middle class of specialists such as merchants, goldsmiths, gem-cutters, stone carvers and painters of books and murals had dwellings more substantial than those of the peasants, but they still fell far short of the opulence of the aristocracy.

The layout and architecture of cities was based on Maya religious beliefs, with distinct astronomical alignments for the major temples and pyramids in virtually every Maya city. The Maya saw their buildings as gigantic living creatures, artificial mountains, which they believed had a life of their own. Because astrology was at the very centre of Maya religious life, we would hardly expect otherwise.

As early as 1921, an archaeologist proposed a correlation between sacred buildings in the city of Uxmal with the 'signs' of the Maya zodiac. Certain interpretations of Maya life are currently being made based on the idea that Maya pyramids and temples, as well as other major buildings, were laid out according to a supposed Maya zodiac. This assumes that the Maya used the same 12 signs of the zodiac as us. Logic would dictate that, as the number 12 is *not* sacred to the Maya, they would be more likely to see either 13 or 20 figures in the night sky, corresponding with their beliefs about sacred numbers. Two damaged pages of the Paris Codex showing a scorpion, a peccary and other indeterminate beings hanging like pendants from the sky-serpent, the Milky Way, indicate that the Maya did indeed have a zodiac, but it notes *13* signs. It is true that the Maya saw several of the constellations as we do: the modern constellation of Scorpio was seen as a scorpion by both the Maya and ourselves, and we know that at the time of the Spanish conquest the Yucatec Maya called the constellation Gemini *Ac,* meaning a peccary. What we see in the Paris Codex are the figures of the zodiac, but not their star patterns, so we cannot accurately claim further correlations with our own zodiac.

Other ancient peoples read vastly different figures in the

sky. Consider the constellation that revolves around the Pole Star. In North America this formation is called the Big Dipper; in Europe it is referred to as the Plough. This grouping is, in fact, also part of a constellation known as the Great Bear. In ancient China, this same grouping was referred to as the Celestial Bureaucrat. We have no reason to believe that the Maya saw the formations in the sky in the same way as ancient Europeans or Egyptians. Another indicator of how figures in the sky are seen, is that rather than seeing a 'man in the moon' the Maya saw a 'rabbit in the moon' as did the ancient Chinese.

A major Maya city such as Tikal typically consisted of a number of stepped platforms topped by masonry structures, all arranged around broad plazas or courtyards. Because many Maya cities were subject to flooding in the wet season, buildings may be grouped in complexes, interconnected by causeways. Dominating the cities are three or four huge temple pyramids built from limestone blocks, over a core of rubble. On the platforms on top of the pyramids, the temples themselves contain one or more corbelled and plaster-covered rooms, but these are so small that they could have been used only on sacred occasions, when their dimensions would admit the few priests who performed rituals not meant for public eyes. To add height and create a more imposing structure, the temples atop the pyramid platforms were themselves heightened by the addition of a roof 'comb'. These imposing and highly ornamented structures, often taller than the temple building itself, were so-named because of their resemblance to the tall, ornamental hair combs worn by Spanish women in formal dress. Their extensive carving and relief work illustrated stories relating to the gods, to Maya mythology, and to the Great Cycles themselves, from which emerged the Prophecy.

However, as imposing as the temples were, the largest structures were invariably what are referred to as 'palaces'. There is considerable debate among archaeologists about the precise use of these large buildings; were they the living quarters of rulers, of the priesthood – or anyone at all? The rooms were small and cramped and, as modern archaeologists have discovered, generally infested with bats. Inscriptions have indicated that they are 'sleeping places', so perhaps, as with such structures in the Southwest of the United States, most of the 'living' was done outdoors and, quite literally, these rooms were used only for sleeping and storage. Another possibility is that the term refers to divination. It was believed that dreams revealed the future, and that the condition of meditative or trance states was a sleep-like state in which the seer was 'dreaming', so these places might have been used by the seers while 'sleeping'. It is also certain that their occupants were part of the ruling elite. The vast majority of the population, the peasant class, lived in small, perishable houses, easily discovered by archaeologists as they were placed on small platforms to elevate them above the level of the annual flooding in the rainy season.

In the central area of major cities would be erected any number of stelae – highly carved standing stones. Usually narrow and more or less rectangular, they stood up to several metres tall and were invariably carved with a standing figure of a richly dressed Maya ruler, almost always carrying some sort of emblematic sign of his office. These stelae reveal the Long Count dates, as they were erected and dated for the purpose of establishing the legitimacy of the ruler illustrated on the stone. In some of the major centres, such as Palenque and Tikal, we have an almost complete list of rulers and dates over the several centuries that stelae were erected using Long Count dates.

Dated stelae are not the only inscriptions to be found in Maya city centres. The walls of temples and other public buildings were often covered with hieroglyphic inscriptions, carvings, paintings and intricate stucco figures. Literally tens of thousands of inscriptions are found within the numerous Maya cities, but it is only within the last ten years, as Maya hieroglyphics begin to be unravelled, that we can take the very first steps toward deciphering them. As with the stelae, many of the hieroglyphic inscriptions appear to relate to the ruling dynasties of the local city.

At Copán, for example, the Temple of the Hieroglyphic Stairway, built in the 8th century AD, contains 63 steps upon which is carved an enormously long text of about 2,500 glyphs, relating the history of the rulers of Copán. We know from this inscription that the 13th ruler of Copán was the person called 18-Rabbit, who took power on 9 July AD 695. Recorded in this inscription are his accomplishments as a builder, and his dedication of temples. We also know from his stela that the Maya were aware that each individual possessed both male and female aspects: 18-Rabbit is depicted in a costume that combines the Jaguar skin kilt with a long skirt, typical of the representation of women on other stelae, thus showing him in his feminine aspect. It is also recorded that on 3 May AD 738 this unfortunate king was captured and beheaded by Cauac-Sky, king of a nearby city, who had heretofore been under the domination of Copán. This defeat was temporary; within a very short time the 14th ruler, Smoke-Monkey, took office. Also recorded are Smoke-Monkey's accomplishments as a builder, and so on, throughout the remaining kings of the Copán dynasties.

Because the Maya cities are part and parcel of the culture and the belief system that produced the Maya Prophecy, let us look briefly at a few of the major cities and some of the architecture relating specifically to the Prophecy.

Tikal

Tikal, in Guatemala, is not only one of the largest Maya cities but also one of the biggest ancient cities in the New World. It is also one of the oldest, and thus one where the first wave of new knowledge, including the Prophecy, took hold. At its peak, the city of Tikal covered 6 square miles and contained about 3,000 buildings, ranging from temples to huts. There are several estimates of population, which vary between 10,000 and 40,000.

There are six huge temple pyramids, the highest of which is 230 feet (70 metres) tall. The centre of Tikal is its great plaza, an entire complex laid out according to the cardinal directions, with huge temple pyramids to both the east and west. To the north is a large acropolis, containing the richly endowed tombs of its rulers. Tikal has some of the finest preserved wooden components of structures found anywhere in the Maya world. Notable are the lintels above the doorways of the temple pyramids, covered with extravagant reliefs of Maya rulers, accompanied by lengthy hieroglyphic texts. Also discovered at Tikal were tombs containing elaborately incised bones, representing Maya gods in various forms of activity. The superb drawing and calligraphy skills exhibited on these give us an idea of what Maya books of that early period might have looked like. One can only wonder at what history and science may have lain within their exquisitely illustrated pages.

A notable feature appearing early on in Maya city architecture was a pyramid complex often referred to as a triadic group: a large temple pyramid flanked by two smaller pyramids, all on the same platform. These are oriented

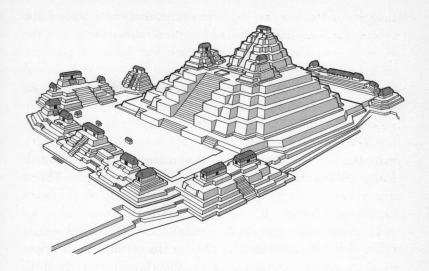

The triadic temple group at Mirador

north–south, and the two smaller pyramids mark the equinox and solstice positions of sunrise, as viewed from the larger pyramid. In general, astronomically oriented architectural complexes are called E complexes, after the first complex to be recognised in group E at Uaxactún. Such complexes also appeared at Tikal and several other cities in the core of the Maya lowlands during the Classic Period.

Another type of pyramid complex which appeared late in the Classic Period at Tikal and a few nearby cities, was the twin pyramid complex. On a square platform oriented to the cardinal directions, a pair of identical pyramids stood along the eastern and western edges. Along the north and south edges stood two other buildings, the south of which was a building with nine doorways, each one an entrance to the nine levels of the Underworld. The two pyramids were truncated, each with a platform on top. They represented the path of the sun, and also suggested the duality present everywhere in the Maya belief. The northern structure was basically an open enclosure like a roofless building, which contained a stela and altar celebrating the current ruler, and placing him in the Overworld or celestial realm.

Palenque

Palenque is considered by some to be the most beautiful of all Maya cities, although in comparison with the huge city Tikal it is very modest in size. To modern students of the Maya Prophecy, Palenque has taken on a rather unbalanced influence, mostly because of the burial there of Lord Pacal, a ruler of the city who died in AD 683. His crypt in the Temple of the Inscriptions made him the Maya equivalent of Tutankhamun. In particular, the large stone slab covering his sarcophagus is elaborately carved, showing a figure of Pacal amid a profusion of Maya symbols. This has been interpreted as everything up to and including it being a picture of an ancient astronaut! There have even been extraordinary interpretations of the lid's significance, based on the fact that two corners of the lid have been chipped off at certain angles. What these interpreters have failed to notice, is that the angles of the chipping correspond exactly to the angles of the corbelled roof that overlies the sarcophagus – clearly the stone lid was slightly too large to be laid down flat, so its corners were chipped off! Nothing more than that.

One of the most genuinely astonishing buildings in the city of Palenque is referred to by its Spanish name – the Temple of the Cross. It was built to celebrate the succession of Chan Bahlum, successor to Pacal, and designed to demonstrate that the succession came under the special auspices of the sun god. As the sun sets on the day of the winter solstice, the only time

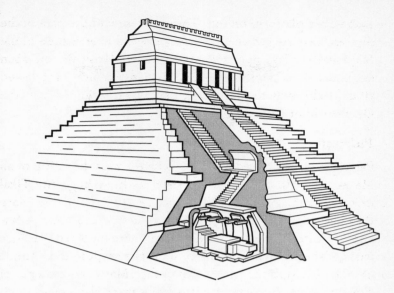

Cross-section view of the Temple of the Inscriptions at Palenque
showing Pacal's tomb

of the year when the temples receive direct sunlight, its rays
pass through a notch in the ridge behind the Temple of the
Inscriptions, falling precisely on and illuminating succession
scenes in the Temple of the Cross. As the sun sinks behind the
ridge, it appears to follow an oblique path along the line of the
stairs to Pacal's tomb, the dying sun symbolically affirming the
succession and then entering the Underworld through Pacal's
tomb. It is the perfect example set in stone of the beliefs of the
Maya about their interactions with the whole of the universe
around them.

Chichén Itzá

The year AD 987 was a pivotal point in the history of the whole
of Mesoamerica, for which the city of Chichén Itzá is a perfect
metaphor. In the century or so previously, the Southern Maya

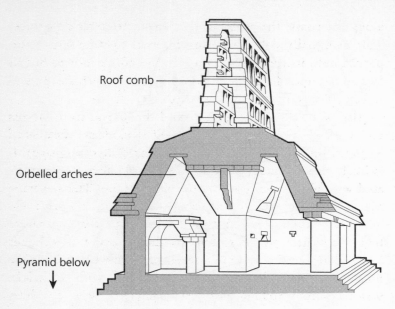

Cross-section of the Temple of the Cross at Palenque

had abandoned their cities in droves, beginning a general migration northward, where new cities were being founded and older cities had a sudden infusion of population. Such was the small town of Uucil-abanal (meaning Seven Bushes). Built in a mountain upland area called the Puuc, an area of fertile soil and rich vegetation, in 987 it stood on the verge of becoming the premier city of Yucatán.

The much older and more highly advanced Toltec were themselves undergoing an upheaval 1,000 miles further north. Shortly after AD 900, the key city of Tula had fallen under the onslaught of a barbarian tribe called the Chichimec. It was, in a sense, the New World equivalent of the fall of Rome. The Toltecs at that time were ruled by a king called Topiltzin, who had taken the title Quetzalcoatl. Driven from his kingdom with his followers, they set sail for lands further east and south along the coast: the realm of the Maya. After his departure, Tula eventually collapsed from internal fighting and disappeared until its rediscovery early in the 20th century. But its legend did not, and all good things in Mesoamerica were said to have flowed from the enlightened city.

Also in AD 987, the Maya record the arrival from 'across the sea' of a man calling himself Kukulcán (Feathered Serpent, the same as Quetzalcoatl in the Toltec language). It is likely that the name Kukulcán became deliberately associated with the ancient god Itzamná at this time. The surviving Maya history of the period recalls Kukulcán as a wise and benevolent ruler. As with all history, we need to remember that it is written by the victors. Within a very short time his forces defeated the Maya in a series of bloody battles; we see images of Maya leaders being sacrificed with Kukulcán benevolently watching the proceedings! It was not long before the balance of the invading Toltec forces found their way to Seven Bushes, at which time it began to be called Chichén. (The Itzá portion of the name became attached in the 13th century, with the arrival of yet a third group of Maya peoples at the site, the Itzá.)

At Chichén Itzá, Kukulcán quickly built a pyramid to himself, still called the pyramid of Kukulcán today, and a major tourist attraction. Because of its construction and orientation, on the solstice the shadow cast by its edge on the stairway of its south side appears to be an undulating snake.

Also at Chichén Itzá is the famous Cenote, the sacred well that is, in fact, a large sinkhole in the limestone bedrock. Throughout Chichén Itzá's history, offerings and sacrifices were thrown into it. Exploration of its depths earlier in the 20th century recovered many artefacts, as well as some human remains.

Maya cities were essentially beliefs set in stone, buildings oriented specifically for their astronomical and astrological significance and use. In a very concrete way, they were the anchors of the Maya Prophecy.

5

Numbers

Numbers were central to the whole of Maya life, sacred, virtually with a life of their own. The Maya number system was the best that existed in the New World until the arrival of Arabic numbers from the Old World. The Maya were capable of incredibly complex calculations that allowed them to construct accurate tables for the prediction of eclipses, the appearance of the Morning and Evening Stars, mathematical tables and to make forecasts and prognostications that would dazzle a modern astrologer. In large part, their achievement resulted from both the form of the Maya numbers and their structure.

It is hard to think of numbers as being 'invented', but someone had to develop the concept of using symbols to represent accumulations of objects. Doubtless, counting was first done on the fingers, giving us the number system based on ten. If we count on our toes also, we have 20 digits, and a number system based on 20: the vestigismal system, as used by the Maya.

Having invented numbers, other uses were discovered for them, apart from the counting of objects and establishing units of value in barter: one squash equals six chillies, and so on. Numbers were soon revealed to be a form of communication often counted as numbers of moons or numbers of days after a certain moon. As people began to live in communities, the need arose to co-ordinate the movements of various groups. Hunters needed to come together for the hunt knowing that game arrived at a certain place at a certain moment; the gatherers needed to know when various berries or nuts were ready to gather; and eventually farmers needed to know when to sow crops. Thus grew the need to measure time.

Before you can measure something, you need to have a means of quantifying it, which is the function of numbers. Without numbers there is no measurement, and in a sense, no time – or at least no way to note the passing of time. And when we begin to note the passing of time, we have invented the calendar. Without a useable number system, an accurate calendar is impossible, and so too is the ability to project knowledge into the future; in other words, to forecast future events, such as the ripening of berries or the expected arrival of herds of game animals at a particular waterhole.

For simple counting any numbers serve the purpose. Addition and subtraction aren't too difficult. If you have a number represented by III, meaning three sheep, and you bring another two into the pen, then you have another II sheep. By simply combining the symbols you get IIIII sheep. And in reverse for subtraction. But what happens when you have a neighbour using your pasture, and each day for IIIIIIIII days he brings in IIIIIIIIIIIIIIII sheep? Now how many are in the pasture? Obviously, there are IIIIIIIII multiplied by IIIIIIIIIIIIIIII sheep. For numbers of any size, and for operations beyond simple addition and subtraction, this system is cumbersome to the point of impossibility. Even in Rome, at the time of the Maya flowering, the number system was difficult to use even for simple operations, and used seven basic symbols: I, V, X, L, C, D and M. It was, in fact, impossible to multiply LIX by CCIII.

This discourse on numbers gives emphasis to the elegant and sophisticated number system used by the Maya. Even to write a number in our 'modern' system, we need ten symbols: 0, 1, 2, 3, 4, 5, 6, 7, 8 and 9. The Maya used only three symbols: a dot, a bar and a stylised seashell.

Wherever the Maya calendar and mathematics originated, it brought a rarity in ancient history — knowledge of the number place system, a major discovery in man's development. For the first time numbers could be manipulated easily, so complex calculations about eclipses and planetary movements became possible. You no longer needed to build a Stonehenge to calculate the date of the next eclipse. You could work out the same thing mathematically on a piece of tree bark with a stick of charcoal. Or, as the Maya came to do, you consulted the appropriate Codex and looked it up in your moon tables, which could be calculated many years in advance. Dates in some Maya texts and inscriptions stretch back many millions of years. These are not pure fantasies: the calendar and the mathematics on which it is based are accurate enough to tell us if and when an eclipse of the moon occurred in 31,412 BC.

Using the three basic symbols — the dot for '1', the bar for '5', and the seashell for '0' — numbers up to 19 could be written simply with bars and dots:

0	1	2	4	5	7	10	18

The Maya number system was based on 20, instead of our decimal system, based on tens. In the first number place, the 'units' column in our system, the Maya number pushed into the next column at 20, in the same way that we move into the '10s' column when it reaches 10. In the '20s' column, it did so when it hit 400, instead of 100 in the decimal system. In addition, numbers in the Maya system are read vertically, with the lowest values, the 'ones' column, at the bottom.

The basic systems look like this:

thousands, etc – hundreds – tens – ones
Tens system

eight thousands, etc
four hundreds 400 x 20
twenties 20 x 20
ones 1 x 20
Maya system

In our decimal system, numbers are sometimes written vertically as well, and are just as readable:

5   We would all read this correctly as 503. Just as we can
0   write our horizontal numbers vertically and still read
3   them, so too did the Maya write their vertical numbers
horizontally from time to time in inscriptions.

Here are some Maya numbers:

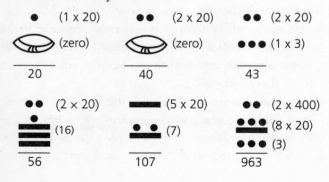

The Maya were among the few ancient peoples to have a concept of 'zero', as shown by the seashell. A number place could be 'empty', like the units column when we reach 10 in the base 10 system.

The sacred nature of Maya numbers is illustrated in a different group of symbols used from time to time in important inscriptions: each number is 'written' as its hieroglyphic god equivalent. This can be just the face of the god or a full figure, as in the following examples (see overleaf). This is a date written in Long Count format from Stela D at Copán, and reads 9.15.5.0.0 10 Ahau 8 Ch'en.

The one flaw in the Maya system is there was no way to express fractions. The Maya knew that the Solar Year was just over 365 days, but they had no way to deal with it in their calendar, at least as a fraction. The Maya calendar was based not on an accumulation of weeks, months, and years, like our system, but as an accumulation of days. These were grouped into a series of hierarchical units, but were still based on numbers of days since the beginning of the Great Cycle and not on their calendar date. A Long Count date, such as 9.15.5.0.0 10 Ahau 8 Ch'en, would be understood as 100,000 or more days since the beginning of the cycle. Other calculations in the tables of the Codices were also calculated on the basis of numbers of days rather than calendar dates. Thus Venus could be expected to appear as the Morning Star every 584 days, rather than every so many months or years. The Day counts over a 5,000-year Great Cycle are obviously huge, so to express them simply and briefly, subdivision units were created (see page 89).

Since fractions were not possible, the Maya used time divisions that could deal with whole numbers where calendar calculation was necessary. For example, the Solar Year was divided into 18 months of 20 days each, giving 360 days,

Maya numbers written as full god-glyphs

with an extra five days 'outside' the calendar, which were thus particularly unlucky.

The Maya had three calendars running simultaneously, each with differing numbers of days and cycles. Because of the complexity of their co-ordination, mathematical tables were constructed, one of which is preserved in the Dresden Codex. They included multiples of 13, 52, 65, 78, and 91. The 13 cycle ran simultaneously with a 20-day cycle in the Ritual Almanac (also called the Sacred Calendar). The 260-day/13-number Ritual Almanac cycle and the 365-day Solar Year coincided only once every 52 years, also calculated as the number of days: 18,980. The nearest whole number to a quarter of the Solar Year was 91; and so on.

Yet other number tables were constructed for the periods of Venus (5 multiplied by 584 days in the Venus cycle = 8 multiplied by 365 = 2,920 days – a calculation accurate to 1 day in 6,000 years). Thus the 8-year Solar/5-year Venus period was considered to be particularly significant astrologically. Lunar tables were also composed. It was discovered that 149 moons equalled 4,400 days, the nearest whole number, so the average lunation for the Maya computations was 29.53020 days, against the actual lunation of 29.53059 days – a miss of only 2.5 minutes a day!

The Dresden Codex also contains eclipse tables, directly connected to the Ritual Almanac. It was discovered that 405 lunations – or 11,980 days – was also equal to 46 260-day Ritual Almanac cycles, again giving a period of particular significance to the Maya. While some Maya rituals are recorded in the Codices, exactly what they were is yet undetermined; many more must have been recorded in the books destroyed by the Spanish.

In fact, it was through the use of Maya eclipse tables that Maya dates were eventually co-ordinated with our own

Gregorian Calendar dates. Maya dates were written using both Long Count dates and Solar Year dates so there is only one possible Solar Cycle that could correspond with a particular 365-day period in the Long Count (remember that the Long Count records the number of elapsed days since the beginning of the Great Cycle). When an eclipse was forecast for a particular day in the Maya calendar, it was discovered that an eclipse had actually happened on that day, which corresponded to 8 November in the Julian Calendar (used in the West at that time). Through a study of our own calendar – which we also inherited from the Egyptians via the Romans – it was a matter of counting back the correct number of days to discover that the Maya Long Count calendar began on 13 August 3114 BC.

The Maya mastery of numbers was not solely confined to astronomy and commerce. Maya architecture was number-driven as well. Buildings were not only aligned to astronomical phenomena and used as observatories, but also expressed numbers in their construction. The Maya daylight realm, the Overworld, was governed by 13 gods (the 13 numbers in the Sacred Calendar), and the night-time world, the Underworld, was governed by nine gods. The numbers nine and 13 were incorporated in virtually every Maya building with a sacred significance. There would be nine or 13 doorways, the stairs would be multiples of nine and 13; or of 20 and 13 to incorporate the 20 days of the Sacred Calendar; or of other numbers and multiples considered sacred, depending on the building's use.

One further note: the Maya possessed a highly sophisticated written language as well. Much of the Prophecy would necessarily have been passed down and preserved in hieroglyphic writing. In a complex series some hieroglyphs represented syllables; some were directly representative pictographs; yet others modified other glyphs. Combined with Maya numbers, it was a particularly effective means of preserving the Prophecy.

Thus we see that the Maya numbers had a highly functional and complex operation, nearly the equal of any modern system, and far in advance of any in use elsewhere in the New World. It allowed the construction and maintenance of a calendar as accurate as anything in use anywhere in the world up until a century or two ago. When the Maya predict that something will occur on a particular date, we may be certain that the mathematics behind it are sound.

6

Calendars

Time

To the Maya, time had an almost physical reality; it was, in a sense, the glue that bound the various dimensions of the universe together. They shared many beliefs about time with the modern world: time does not stand still; time can be measured; and time flows away from the past towards the future. Further, time can be divided into 'hierarchical' units that can be used for mathematical calculations: to know how much time has passed, and to predict the timing of future events. Or, these units can be used to determine when a particular event occurred relative to other events, or to the current time.

Time was seen as circular and cyclical; the events which occur in one cycle of time will recur in the next cycle. It was, surprisingly, a view of time not altogether different from that held by Einstein or of Eastern religions, which talk of the Wheel of Karma. It is a linking together of past, present and future events. The past is a clue to the present, and both past and present can be used to look into the future. Perhaps a modern Westerner might say that those who fail to learn the lessons of the past are doomed to repeat them. That we uniformly almost fail to do so is, perhaps, a reflection of our Western belief that time is linear rather than circular.

Also reflected in the Maya calendar and mathematics are both mystic and mythical aspects. What we consider 'mythical' had a concrete reality to the Maya; there was absolutely no difference between 'mythical' and 'reality'. The Maya acknowledged an unseen world of forces and energies influencing daily as well as long-term community life. It is surely our loss that we do not.

For the Maya, the relationship between cyclical time, its units and the supernatural, readily added the quality of divination to their understanding of time. In a sense then, the Maya inhabited an ongoing and continuous world of prophecy. Thus the Maya Prophecy is far from a unique occurrence; it was a natural part of everyday Maya life.

All of the Maya beliefs and ideas about time came together and culminated in the Maya calendar. Far from being just a simple device to distinguish one day from the next, it is a complex synthesis of a number of different cycles, all running at the same time and each keeping track of the passage of time in different ways. Each cycle has its associated deities, overlapping and penetrating each other. The various cycles of the calendar also overlap the four quarters of the universe and interconnect with each of the cycles. In addition, each part of the calendar can influence each other part.

The religious associations of the calendar are clearly demonstrated in Classic Period inscriptions, where both the numbers and the units of the Long Count are represented by glyphs that are portraits of deities. They are clearly personified, not abstractions like our own numbers and calendar units. In the earliest forms of these glyphs, the deity is seen as a full portrait, carrying the number or unit on his back. Thus the process of divination becomes incredibly complex.

The Long Count Calendar

Long-term cycles, like the Great Cycles of the Suns and dates across the whole range of Maya history, were fixed according to what is referred to as the Long Count calendar, which began on 13 August 3114 BC. As with our own calendar, the Long Count calendar was not used just to keep track of days and predict days' positions, but also to record past events, relationships between those events in terms of their time occurrence, and the understanding of the patterns of those events. It also must be recognised that the Maya did not think of 'historical events' in the same way as us. 'History', as the Maya understood it, was not recorded in order to establish the accurate representation of events, but was principally used for the purposes of divination and often to establish the legitimacy of the lineage of the local ruler. To this end 'historical events' were often altered or manufactured. (This, of course, has absolutely no counterpart in modern times!) In one instance, a counterfeit stela has been discovered featuring alterations and invented birth dates and lineage for a particular ruler. Presumably this stela was 'discovered' around the time of his accession and used to 'prove' the legitimacy of his reign.

All Maya calendars, including the Long Count calendar, use the day as the elementary unit, a *kin* in Maya. The Maya day began at sunset, and continued until sunset the following day. Each day had its associated god, who 'took over' at sunset from the god of the previous day. Night was more sacred than day, and it was believed to be the time that the gods were closest to men. The Long Count is based on several subdivisions, and is written as an accumulation of various time periods, each measured in days. The basic component of the Long Count is the *tun*, a period of 360 days. It is the nearest to the 365-day Solar Calendar or Vague Year that can be computed in 20-day units. A *tun* is made up in turn of 18 *unials*, each of which contains 20 *kins* (or days). Going the other way, 20 *tuns* constitute a *katun*, and 20 *katuns* in turn make up a *baktun*, the largest unit of the Long Count.

1 *kin*	= 1 day	
20 *kins*	= 1 *unial*	(20 days)
18 *unials*	= 1 *tun*	(360 days)
20 *tuns*	= 1 *katun*	(7,200 days = 20 × 360-day years, or about 19.7 × 365.25-day years)
20 *katuns*	= 1 *baktun*	(144,000 days = 400 × 360-day years or about 394 × 365.25-day years)

Using these units in combination, a Long Count date was written as an accumulation of days since the beginning of the current Great Cycle in 3114 BC. The first number of the date was the number of elapsed baktuns. Most Maya inscriptions from the lowlands, where the Long Count was primarily used, fall in *baktun* 8. The second component was the number of katuns elapsed in the current baktun, the third was the number of tuns, and so on. It is specifically these types of Long Count calculations upon which the Maya Prophecy is based.

The oldest dated monument so far discovered is a stela at Chiapa de Corzo, a major ceremonial centre. It is dated in the Long Count calendar, corresponding to 7 December 36 BC. Evidence that the Maya inherited the Long Count calendar from elsewhere arises as monuments bearing the oldest

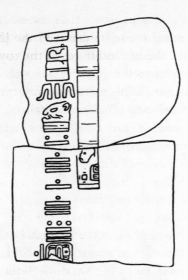

7 baktuns = 7 x 144,000 = 1,008,000 days
16 katuns = 16 x 7,200 = 115,200 days
6 tuns = 6 x 360 = 2,160 days
16 uinals = 16 x 20 = 320 days
18 kins 18 x 1 = 18 days
Total of 1,125,698 days

A long count date, written as 7. 16. 6. 16. 18, and corresponding
to a date in 31 BC

Long Count dates appear outside the Maya region.
Archaeologist Michael Coe states: 'The "Maya" calendar had
reached what was pretty much its final form by the 1st
Century BC among peoples who were under powerful Olmec
influence and who may not even have been Maya.'

Dated monuments may appear in certain areas and not
others as they were used principally to establish the legitimacy of ruling dynasties. In areas without such dating, it is
quite likely that there were no hereditary ruling classes, for

whom 'legitimacy' was an issue. Coe states: 'By the time the Long Count calendar made its debut in the [Maya] lowlands . . . about AD 250, the life and times of the royal house had to be the major preoccupation of the Maya state, and full Maya civilisation had begun.' This raises two other questions about the Long Count calendar. Why was it used exclusively for royalty, and why did it start 3,000 years before a royal line emerged? The answer would appear to be that it dates to the 'birth of the gods', as indicated by the inscription at Palenque (page 54), an attempt to legitimise the ruler by indicating his ancient lineage to 'the gods' themselves. Could it have been calculated backwards to 3114 BC? There is no reason why not, given the state of Maya mathematics. But why a date that falls virtually at the start of other Old World civilisations?

The Long Count calendar was abandoned, at least for inscriptions, in about the 10th century AD. This period corresponds with the abandonment of Southern Maya cities and the general movement northwards. Its disappearance indicates not a disappearance of the beliefs associated with it, but rather the need to use Long Count inscriptions for dynastic legitimacy. This situation most likely came about because the dynasties were overthrown and a ruling class that had no need to prove its legitimacy came to power: the Toltecs, who dominated Maya life after the 10th century. They had legitimacy simply because they had the strongest military position. Though it no longer appears in inscriptions, the Long Count calendar is, in fact, still in use in some Maya areas today.

The Sacred Calendar or Ritual Almanac

The Sacred Calendar of the Maya is called the Ritual Almanac. It was a cycle of 260 days, and was (and still is) mainly used for religious purposes, divination and as the chief guide to ceremonial activity. In turn it is composed of two smaller interlocking cycles, one comprising 20 days, each with its own overseeing god, and the other comprising 13 numbers. Each of the 20 days had its own name, so any day in the 20-day cycle could be designated by both a number and a name. For example, the first day of the cycle was named Imix, so the first day of the cycle would be designated 1 Imix. The second day of the cycle was named Ik, and thus would be numbered 2 Ik. The 13th day of the cycle was named Ben, and would be designated 13 Ben. By the 14th day of the cycle, Ix, all of the 13 numbers were used up, so the number cycle started again: 1 Ix. And so on, recycling each of the 13 numbers through the remainder of the 20 days. But when the 20 days were completed, with 7 Ahau, and the 20-day cycle began again with Imix, only 7 of the 13 numbers had been used up, so the designation of the 21st day of the cycle was 8 Imix, the 22nd day was 9 Ik, and so on. 1 Imix would not appear again until the 261st day, thus completing the 260-day cycle.

The 13-number, 20-day cycle

1 Imix	1 Ix	1 Manik
2 Ik	2 Men	2 Lamat
3 Akbal	3 Cib	and so on...
4 Kan	4 Caban	
5 Chicchan	5 Etz' Nab	
6 Cimi	6 Caucac	
7 Manik	7 Ahau	
8 Lamat	8 Imix	
9 Muluc	9 Ik	
10 Oc	10 Akbal	
11 Chuen	11 Kan	
12 Eb	12 Chicchan	
13 Ben	13 Cimi	

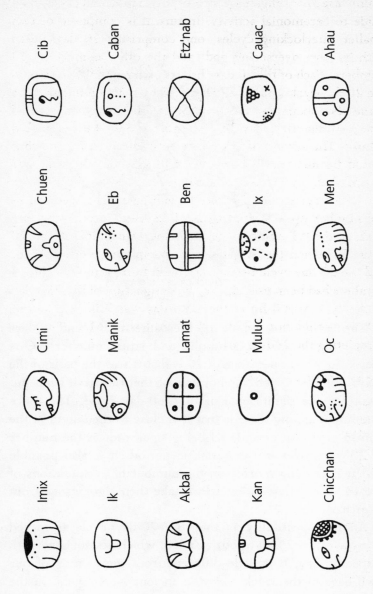

Name glyphs of Ritual Almanac days

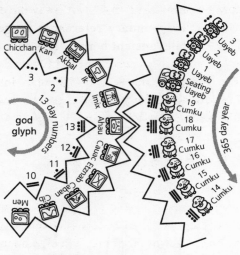

The Ritual Almanac   The 'Vague Year'

The three interlocking calendar cycles
showing the date 13Ahau 18Cumku

Throughout the whole of Mesoamerica 13 and 20 are considered important symbolic and ritual numbers. One reason for the importance of 20 is that it was the basis of the Maya number system. A number of theories have been put forth for the significance of the 260-day cycle. The more prominent among these is that it is close to the length of the human gestation period, 13 being significant as the number of 20-day cycles in the gestation period. It is also possible that it is nothing more than the number of permutations of the 13 and 20 day cycles, which take their significance from elsewhere.

Another possibility is that the 20-day cycle is sacred because of the 20 'day gods', each of which is associated with a specific day. It is little different from the naming of our own days of the week after the ancient Norse gods. In the case of the Maya, however, the 'gods' may have been a little nearer to home. Fragmentary references suggest they may have been real people, ancient heroes. It is even possible that they were the 'gods' who accompanied Quetzalcoatl.

Whatever its origin, the Sacred Calendar, in combination with the Long Count calendar, are the basis upon which the timing of the Prophecy is calculated.

The Solar Calendar or Vague Year

The third calendar cycle, also referred to as the Vague Year, corresponds to the 365-day solar year, but ignores the extra day needed at leap year. It is likely that the Maya knew this, but as the Long Count and the Ritual Almanac were the central calendars it simply was not that important. It comprises 18 months of 20 days each, along with an additional five-day period to make up the total of 365 days. Each month is named, and each of the days are designated by number. The first day of the month is the '0' day, referred to as the 'seating' day. For example, the first month of the Maya calendar is called Pop, so the first day of Pop is actually transcribed as 'the seating of Pop', in essence, the day in which the day-god Pop settles into his new routine for that month. According to Maya philosophy, the influence of any particular time span starts before the actual time span, and persists beyond its apparent ending. Thus the 20th day of the month of Pop is designated 19 Pop, followed on the succeeding day by the seating of the next month god, Uo. And again this follows through for 20 days until 19 Uo, the day after which becomes the seating of the next month god Zip, and so on, throughout the year. At the 360th day, 19 Cumku, comes the five-day period called Uayeb, which is considered particularly unlucky.

The month glyphs

The Calendar Round: Relating the Calendars

Because more than one cycle is running – the number/day cycle of the Ritual Almanac and the 365-day cycle of the Solar Calendar – any given day will normally have two 'dates': its Solar Calendar designation and its Ritual Almanac designation. The start of the two will correspond only once in every 52 years. This period is called the Calendar Round, a highly sacred period of time. The end of each 52-year cycle is celebrated with New Fire rituals. Pyramids were refaced with stone, adding another layer (which also gives us a way of dating pyramids, like counting the rings in a tree), houses were pulled down and rebuilt, and there was a general refurbishment of the entire material culture. It was seen as a time of the dying of the old and the rebirth of the new.

The Ritual Almanac was basic to the culture of every Central American and Mexican Indian group until the time of the Spanish conquest. It is the oldest discovered part of the calendar, having come into use well before 500 BC. The names and attributes of the various parts of the calendar also seem fairly uniform throughout the various cultures. The 365-day Vague Year Solar cycle is also a basic feature of all of the Mexican and Central American cultures, and is equally ancient. Its first documented appearance comes slightly later, but every pre-Columbian group used some version of it. Unlike the Ritual Almanac, the Solar Calendar varied considerably in the month names and attributes from culture to culture. It survives today in some areas of Maya Mexico.

The Aztec Calendar Stone

Other Mesoamerican people had beliefs in Great Cycles, the

Suns, most notably the Aztecs, further north. They preserved yet another ancient 'document' relating to the periods of the five suns: the Aztec Sun Stone. The Aztecs shared the same cosmology as the Maya, as well as similar beliefs about the cyclic nature of life. It is virtually certain, as we have seen, that both the Aztec and Maya beliefs came from the same, older, source.

On the Calendar Stone, the most remote of the Aztec Suns is represented by Ocelotonatiuh, the jaguar god: 'during that Sun lived the giants that had been created by the gods but were finally attacked and devoured by jaguars'. The Second Sun is signified by the head of Ehecoatl, the god of the air: 'During that period the human race was destroyed by high winds and hurricanes and men were converted into monkeys.' The symbol of the Third Sun is a head representing rain and celestial fire: 'In this epic everything was destroyed by a rain of fire from the sky and the forming of lava. All the houses were burnt. Men were converted into birds to survive the catastrophe.' The Fourth Sun is represented by Chalchihutlicue, the water goddess: 'destruction came in the form of torrential rains and flood. The mountains disappeared and men were transformed into fish'.

On the Calendar Stone the symbol of our current epoch, the Fifth Sun, is the face of Tonatiuh, the sun god. He appears with the symbol *ollin*, which represents movement. The Fifth Sun is known as the Sun of Movement, so called because in the ancient Aztec records it is said: 'there will be a movement of the earth and from this we shall all perish'.

If this Prophecy is true, what can we do about it – if anything?

EXERCISE

Visualisations succeed for some levels of work, but at

other times physical action is necessary.

Cyclic time, the various cycles that the Maya lived by, are ultimately the cycles and rhythms and patterns of nature. Rhythm and cycle and pattern are fundamental to all life – the life of the stars and planets, of animals and plants, of you and me, of the universe itself. It might be said that they are life itself. The Maya understood that on Earth we also experience rhythm as duality: positive and negative, light and dark, male and female, good and bad, and so on. Our own everyday lives move in a number of patterns and rhythms. Some are biological, some are psychological and some are developmental, each cycle leading us further along the path to self-realisation. The psychological and developmental cycles are often the most difficult, requiring us at each stage to confront our fears and insecurities, all part of the rhythms and cycles of growth common to both man and the universe. Rhythm is the connecting thread that weaves all levels of life into One.

☆ To see the cycles and patterns in your own life, you need to make three lists: *Relationships*, *Career* and *Money*. Under each, write down in chronological order significant events or turning points in each category.

☆ Under *Relationships*, write down all of your past and present relationships, and how each developed.

☆ Under *Career*, list the jobs you wanted but failed to get, and each job you did. For each job in both categories, list what you wanted or expected or hoped for from each, whether it went right or wrong, and how.

☆ Under *Money*, look at both your spending and earning habits. Does money go as fast as you get it? Do you hoard it 'just in case'? Is there ever enough?

Take plenty of time on this – you don't have to get it all down in one sitting. An experience does not necessarily recur at exactly the same time. What we are looking for is the repeat of patterns, such as the point in a new relationship where we realise we've done it again! These are the markers, the pointers to unfinished experiences, unlearned lessons. They are the pattern of our own, personal prophecy.

7

Understanding and Preparing for the Times Ahead

At first glance the religious beliefs of a people who practised human sacrifice would appear to have little to teach us about how to live our own lives more fully and how to deal with events to come. The Maya were, in fact, more in touch with the full and rich realities of life than we can ever hope to be in the narrow confines of our Western social and belief systems.

A Taoist or a Shinto would be much better placed philosophically and psychologically to understand the Maya thought process, which bears certain similarities to Shintoism. The Maya understand that the universe is a single unitary form, and that the physical world is both intertwined with and interpenetrates other levels of being.

The supernatural, the incorporeal, and experience beyond the usual five senses were a part of normal everyday experience, simply representing other dimensions of reality. Physical boundaries – of one's own body, of plants and animals, of stones, and even of the planet itself – were not really limits, but were only transitions between the Heavens

and the Underworld. Time and space were seen as insepara-
ble and complementary components of the universe.
Lifeforce was everywhere, penetrating everything, including
that which the Western world would perceive as inanimate:
stones, buildings, mountains and the physical earth itself.
Thus the Maya process of divination was not one of merely
fortune-telling, but of striving to put one's self in harmony
with the flow of the entire universe.

The Maya also perceived a range of supernatural entities
inhabiting various dimensions of time and space: deities,
symbolic flora and fauna, and masses of minor spirits, who all
had connections with one or more regions of the universe,
especially the cardinal directions or with specific units of
time. They were not limited by these however, because all of
the universe was continuous and interpenetrating, its inhabitants at all levels constantly moving through the time/space
continuum.

The Maya perfectly understood the esoteric truism 'as
above, so below': all levels of reality, from the smallest to
the largest, are reflections of each other. For example,
reflecting their belief that the sky is held up by a god at each
of its four corners, the cardinal directions, the house with its
four corners may symbolise the universe itself. What happens
within that house, then, should reflect the harmony and
order of the universe. It is hardly a flawed concept. Similarly
a maize field with its four corners, or the community itself,
held up by its 'pillars', should likewise reflect the harmony
and order of the universe. It would seem that modern
communities could learn much here. Equally, cosmic scales
and distances could be reduced to earthly proportions both as
a means of comprehending them and to find unity with them.
Maya cities were laid out on this basis, and so were groups of
buildings within them, such as the E groups of temples.

This understanding is also reflected in Maya ritual, where the same ritual may be performed for an individual, the community, or the cosmos itself – a recognition that one is a reflection at a different scale of the others. The Maya lived their lives with the knowledge that, because life is cyclic, all that is done in the earthly realm will be destroyed and rebuilt in the next Great Cycle. The New Fire ceremonies at the end of each 52-year Calendar Round cycle, acted out on a small scale the rebuilding of the world after the end of the last Great Cycle – and the next, the fulfilment of the Prophecy. It was a sweeping away of the old and the rebirth of the new, true for individuals as well as societies.

All of this, including the Great Cycles, is part of a yet larger picture, a deep understanding of the need for balance and harmony in all things. Imbalance and discord were believed to be at the root of all ills – individual, social, even planetary. The calendar cycles and mathematics were essential ingredients in the greater picture. Because of this understanding, the whole of Maya civilisation was geared to maintaining moderation and balance, even to the balancing of the gift of life itself. All life was seen to be the gift and granting of the gods, therefore it was necessary to give life in return to balance the equation. Blood was believed to be the embodiment of life itself, and thus an appropriate gift to the gods to balance the gift of life. An individual balanced his own life through ritual bloodletting, and the community balanced its life through ritual human sacrifice. Something small could represent something large in the greater scheme of things, so the release of an individual's blood through sacrifice could represent the blood of the whole community. Because the lives of the nobles and rulers were of greater 'cosmic' value, the sacrifice of a ruler was a particularly potent offering. Hence ritual warfare to capture another city's ruler.

In virutally all modern religious beliefs the idea of sacrifice is embodied. The willingness to give up one's life, either ritually through service or in some cases literally, is seen as the highest spiritual act. So the Maya sacrifices were not always unwilling by any means. The Maya called them a sacrifice; we call them heroes.

'Everyday' beliefs centred around day-to-day events, and there was little belief that the events of this life affected the afterlife, although they could create imbalance or disharmony. This could take much undoing in the afterlife – the Maya equivalent of Karma. Maya beliefs about the afterlife were similar to Egyptian ones. The departed soul took a difficult journey through the Underworld, outwitting the Nine Gods of Death, like Xbalanque and Hunahpu in the *Popol Vuh*. Those who successfully completed this journey were lifted into the sky to become stars. Just as the Egyptians equated the life cycle with the rise and fall of the Nile, the Maya equated it with the life cycle of maize.

The Maya Gods

It is difficult to make a definitive list of the many Maya gods. As the Maya concept of the supernatural saw many interacting and inter-combining forces and energies, any single god at any single place in time/space was a specific combination of various forces and energies. If one of the aspects of time/space or other forces changed somewhat, a new portrayal emerged. Much archaeological evidence supports this idea, in that many images and text references blend together the names, titles, emblems and characteristics of other deities.

Significant within this was the portrayal of those deities in a mixture of colours, which may have provided a visual clue to which dimension of the deities was represented. For example, the more it featured the colour red, the more the deity would take on characteristics of the east. Thus a god was never a separate entity, but a coalesced portion of total reality interpenetrated by and interpenetrating the rest of creation. For example, the Skybearer, Pauahtun, if he appeared in the east, would take on some of the characteristics of the east. If he appeared in the south, he would take on some of the characteristics of the south. If Venus was at its apex at the same time, he would take on some of its characteristics too. A particular point of the sacred calendar would dictate yet further aspects. Thus Pauahtun was not just 'a god'. We cannot put him in a list of gods defined by immutable characteristics. Core characteristics and features existed, but rarely in a pure form. It is rather like the shades and tints of a colour. There is a very specific colour called 'yellow', but we mostly see it in its many variations. The Maya gods are perceived in the same way.

Maya gods also had male or female counterparts, and often their young or old versions. This was an inherent and deliberate recognition of the duality of all nature: hot/cold, up/down, left/right, good/bad, and so on. For example, **Ix Chel**, the old lunar goddess, was the wife and counterpart of Itzamná, often depicted as Kinich Ahau, the sun god. She represented the mature, grandmotherly attributes of nurturing and caring in the human, feminine aspect, midwifery and the aide of new birth in all its forms. In her duality, it was understood that too much nurturing becomes domineering and smothering. In her younger aspect, she is Ix Ch'up, representing the same characteristics of nurturing and caring, as would a young woman.

If we understand that Itzamná was the Great God, of which all other gods were a part, then certainly **Kinich**

Ahau was a dimension of Itzamná, as, indeed, were all other gods. His principal attribute was the deep, accumulated wisdom of the ages. In his duality, it is understood that wisdom must be brought to the people in digestible form; wisdom for its own sake is worthless.

Other Maya gods were also representative of desirable human attributes. For example, Pauahtun the skybearer, who held up the sky, was an equivalent of Atlas, except he held the sky rather than the Earth on his shoulders. His attributes were: the bearer of heavy loads, endurance, solidity, strength; in his duality, he could become stubborn and self-limiting.

Other important gods included:

Chac, the god of rain and lightning, the nurturer of all of nature and the sustainer of life. In his duality, too much rain brought the flood, the destroyer of life.

Hun Nal, the maize god, the material sustainer of human life. But the duality of maize is that if it were treated carelessly, it would decay.

Yum Cimih, the lord of death, who cleared away the old and that which has served its purpose, roughly equivalent to the Hindu god Shiva. In his duality, it was recognised that something incomplete or with unfulfilled purpose could be removed prematurely.

Huracán, the god of violent and sudden change, from whom we get our word 'hurricane'. That which appeared to be a disaster may in the end bring greatest benefit. He challenged us to look beyond appearances. In his duality, he reminded us to use caution against destructiveness with no purpose of renewal behind it.

Xbalanque and **Hunahpu**, the hero twins of the *Popol Vuh*, represented the classic hero: he or she who journeys forth, meets difficult challenges, and brings back a boon for his or her fellow men. They are a constant reminder of the necessity for a heroic approach to life, but their duality reminds us that the person who ventures forth and brings back something that serves only themselves, is no hero at all.

Preparations: A New Frame of Mind

The Maya gods and their dualities teach us some answers. Huracán teaches us the duality of disaster – that it may open the door to an even better future – and Xbalanque and Hunahpu teach us to have a heroic approach to life. All of the gods teach us of the nature of nature, and our oneness with and inner reflection of it.

If the Maya Prophecy foretells the return of a major comet that has brought catastrophic change when fragments of it impacted on the Earth, what can be done about it? The Maya and their gods teach us that this is an act of nature. These acts of nature are mostly remembered worldwide as flood stories. Each one relates how in some manner the people living at the time had abandoned their connection with the natural world around them, and developed a lifestyle out of harmony with it. Those who were saved – the Noahs – still had, in some way, maintained their inner connection to the flow of the world around them – *of which the occasional celestial event is a component part*. Because the human race is an integral part of nature, at least when it permits itself to be, the warning of impending events is virtually in-built. The exercises in this book thus emphasise a reconnection to the deepest, most connected part of ourselves. If there is an upcoming event, those who are connected will *know* where to be and what to do.

For many over-intellectualised and compulsively analytical Westerners, this answer may seem inadequate or ridiculous.

Chac   Itzamná   Kinich
                                Ahau

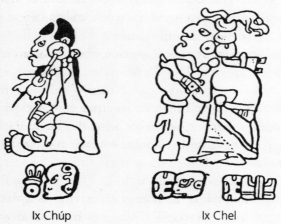

Ix Chúp   Ix Chel

Some gods of the Maya pantheon with their name glyphs,
from the Dresden Codex

This reaction illustrates precisely the point as above – inner connection to nature is *not* a function of the intellect, but occurs deep inside. The only function of the intellect is to note the connection and make decisions based on that connection, not to figure out the connection itself. Connection is an *experience*, not a thought.

The exercises here help start the process of reconnection, the individual's best hope of dealing with what is ahead.

EXERCISE: RECONNECTION

Reconnecting to nature is a very practical experience. As we open ourselves to deeper levels of our own being, we also begin to attune ourselves to our own natural cycles and rhythms of life. In doing so, we like-wise begin to become aware of the pulse of all life around us. Many of you already have a high attunement to nature; it is perhaps through this attunement that you began to realise that your own life exists beyond the boundaries of your physical body.

This attunement exercise takes place over an entire year.

☆ First, find a favourite tree in a place where you are comfortable meditating, away from the hurly-burly of everyday life. Sit with your back to the tree, and close your eyes.

☆ Allow yourself to 'melt into' the tree – as if the two of you are one. Eventually you will become aware of the lifeforce of the tree, which will become a very distinct sensation the longer you experience it.

☆ As you begin to experience the tree's lifeforce, sit

facing each of the four cardinal directions in turn, taking the time to attune to the tree each time. Be aware of how the lifeforce varies, depending on the direction you are facing. This was noticed, and indeed revered, by the Maya. The spring or summer is the best time to start this exercise, when the lifeforce is at its strongest. Take a tape recorder with you, or a notebook to record your experiences for comparison with later experiences.

☆ Revisit the same tree and repeat the process at the turning of each season, just as the leaves are turning in the autumn, when the tree is barren in the winter, as it is budding in the spring, when the tree is in the fullness of life in the summer. You will be amazed at the differences, and at your own ability to clearly distinguish them. It is this degree of sensitivity to nature and to ourselves that we are striving to develop as a way of reconnecting to the natural world around us. It is our inner voice that is one with nature that will clearly guide us through whatever lies ahead, whether it involves a celestial event or not.

EXERCISE: FINDING THE HERO INSIDE YOURSELF

The hero twins Xbalanque and Hunahpu are the Maya archetypes of the universal hero figure. All spiritual growth requires the seeker to undertake a quest into the Underworld, as did they. The Underworld for each of us, personally, is often called the Shadow-Self, the place where all of our deepest fears are buried. Personal growth is a journey into that Underworld, to confront and work through those fears.

The first and greatest heroic act is the willingness to

undertake the process of personal growth, to be willing to take down the barriers between who you have become and who you really are. Truly there is no way for you to fully anticipate who you might become through the awakening process. That, too, is a fear we must confront.

In this exercise, you will meet a strong and wise Being. It is important to remember that the person you are meeting is yourself. This is not some disincarnate entity, not a spirit guide, not a person outside yourself. It is a projection of the formless Being at the deepest level of your own heart, where your inner strengths lie. It is the person that you have the potential to become, a person in full manifestation of their own humanity.

☆ To begin, close your eyes and find yourself back at the sacred pathway leading to your pyramid. It is night, you are dressed in initiation robes, and are accompanied by the High Priest or Priestess.

☆ The High Priest or Priestess, your external teachers, can accompany you only so far on your journey. Then you must walk your path alone. They will walk with you only so far as you start this journey toward the pyramid.

☆ As you reach the stairs up the pyramid, the High Priest or Priestess offers their blessing, and you proceed alone. You climb the pyramid, and enter the inner chamber.

☆ The chamber is lit by a single candle, and there is a

stone bench against the right-hand wall of the chamber, where you sit down.

☆ When you are ready, a shimmering light will gradually appear along the wall opposite you. As the light brightens, a human form will appear within it. Dressed as a Maya warrior, or in some other appropriate costume, this figure embodies your deepest strengths – the hero within. Strength radiates from this figure, a tangible strength you can feel. Know that this strength is yours, and you can draw on it whenever you wish. You can also converse with this figure, and receive guidance and direction from it. This figure may guide you on ways to draw on your inner strength, or you may receive reassurance of its continuing presence no matter what. Or, it may have yet other guidance or direction for you.

☆ When you feel complete with the experience, the figure will fade. Arise from your bench and return to the stairs down the pyramid. When you are ready, descend to the sacred pathway and the point of your departure. Take a few deep breaths, and become aware of your external surroundings again. When you are ready, your eyes will come open naturally.

EXERCISE: FINDING THE BARRIERS TO THE NATURAL YOU

This is a lengthy meditation, but it is a major one that can be used time and time again to uncover increasingly subtle blockages that keep us separated from the Source of our Being. The Maya recognised the manifold nature of reality and the individual. In this meditation we use the four cardinal directions and their colours to reveal our inner need for growth. This meditation uses the inner sanctum of the pyramid as a metaphor for the deepest inner self, where all blockages become visible. The sacred chamber at the top of our pyramid in this meditation is square, with a door in the centre of each wall, which leads to the temple platform on which it rests. Each wall of the chamber is a different colour, relating to the direction it faces. Each direction has its particular meaning, and as you face each direction, some of that meaning may express itself in what is revealed to you. In the exact centre is a square stone bench, with each side facing one of the four doors. This visualisation will move counter-clockwise, as the Maya understood the world to move.

☆ Close your eyes and find yourself standing at the start of the processional way leading to the stairs of the pyramid. When you are ready, the moment has come to start your journey.

☆ You reach the pyramid, and climb to the top, where you enter the sacred chamber. You sit facing East, the direction of the new entering your life, of expansion and new birth. The wall is painted red, and is lit by a single red-burning candle, bathing the chamber in soft red light.

☆ In the wall is a doorway. From this doorway will emerge a red figure that is you in Maya dress representative of your need at that moment. This red figure will show you in some appropriate way where certain of your inner barriers lie, and may have something to tell you or show you about yourself. He or she may offer suggestions about how to begin to dismantle the barriers at that level of your being.

☆ When it has done all that is necessary, it will depart. Make a clear intention to remember what it has shown you, and then turn to the doorway on your left, facing North, the direction of the ancestral dead and of wisdom. The wall is white, lit with a colourless, burning candle.

☆ Your white Maya self will now appear. Again, there will be something shown you about yourself. When it has done all that is necessary, it will depart. Make a clear intention to remember what it has shown you.

☆ Then turn to the doorway on your left, facing West.

☆ The wall is black, and there is no candle to illuminate this wall. It is the direction of the subconscious, the shadow self, and of death and sacrifice. Your black Maya self will appear, visible even against the black. It will impart information as before.

☆ When you are complete with your black Maya self, turn to the left again, to face the South. The wall is yellow, and illuminated by a yellow-burning candle. This direction represents the richness of life, abundance and fulfilment. Your yellow Maya self will appear. It too, will have something to show you about yourself.

☆ When you are complete with your yellow Maya self, it will exit. Take a moment to recall all that your Maya selves have imparted. When you feel complete with the process, begin to descend the route you came up, until you are again standing at the start of the processional way.

☆ Take a few deep breaths, and become aware of your surroundings again. When you are ready, your eyes will come open naturally.

EXERCISE: THE 'SLEEPING PLACE'

The most serious flaw in the Maya world-view developed through increasing contact with, and eventual conquest by, the Toltecs, who, by that time, had drifted far from the positive influences of Quetzalcoatl/Kukulcán/Itzamná. The emphasis shifted from oneness with nature and connection to the Earth, and focused instead on the sky, where lived terrible and hostile gods that needed to be placated on a regular basis with blood. With dire consequences, the Maya eventually lost contact with the positive and nurturing forces of nature. As have we.

This is an exercise designed to help you connect with the female, nurturing, Mother Earth dimension of the godhead. In the West most of us are conditioned to experience God as separate from ourselves, and ourselves from other people and things. When we begin to address God as 'mother', the all-embracing, there is a subtle inner shift that increases our awareness of our oneness with all.

The Maya used the term 'sleeping' to denote a trance-like state in which the seer or shaman was in intimate contact with other dimensions of reality. The place where this was done, either the temple or the sacred precinct of the pyramid, was referred to as the 'sleeping place'. Here we are going to use the dream state as a point of contact. It is time when our subconscious is nearer the surface, and our unhealthy conditioning can be made more easily visible.

In this exercise your own bed becomes the temple platform on top of a Maya pyramid. If you have a small glass or crystal pyramid, it can be placed beneath your pillow or under the bed to reinforce the image.

☆ As you fall asleep, visualise the pyramid beneath you, and Earth goddess, Mother Earth, overlighting your bed and your dreams. Ask to be shown something to bring you closer to Earth goddess awareness within yourself. Remember that what you are really invoking is a closer connection to the natural world of which you are a part.

☆ When you are awake, be aware of the times you think of, or speak to, God. If you are from a God-the-Father background, address your thoughts and prayers first to 'Father', and then address the same thoughts or prayers to 'Mother'. Be aware of your own responses first of all, and then of the response of the world to those thoughts or prayers. It will surprise you.

EXERCISE: EXPERIENCING ITZAMNÁ

The Maya fully understood the oneness of all creation, both on the earth and beyond. This 'Great God' was symbolised through the form of Itzamná. When we too understand the oneness of all things, including the rhythms and cycles of the cosmos that affect life on Earth, we can fully attune ourselves to them. From this oneness will come, ultimately, all answers that we seek.

☆ To start, close your eyes and find yourself again standing at the start of the processional way leading to the pyramid. You are dressed in heavy initiation robes, for it is the hour before sunrise. The jungle air has a chill.

☆ As you walk alone towards the pyramid, you are aware of the soft, slightly damp breeze through the jungle, and, with the exception of the sound of your sandals on the stone pathway, the utter stillness.

☆ You reach the stairs of the pyramid, and climb to the sacred chamber on top. It is dimly lit. As you walk further inwards, you reach the doorway to the sanctuary and enter. At the far side of this chamber is a window, looking east. There is a stone bench in the exact centre, where you sit facing the window.

☆ To the east, the first blush of impending sunrise colours the horizon. To the west, a few bright stars are still visible in the inky black sky. As the light grows and spreads, the jungle below you becomes visible, soon followed by the patchwork fields of the milpas that surround the temple city.

☆ At the instant of sunrise, there is a surge of lifeforce through you and throughout the world around you — the force that connects all levels of life. Feel your oneness with that force, and your oneness with all that you behold from your vantage point. Know that all life is one, and that you are part of that oneness. And, that there is a knowing, conscious purpose to all that you are one with. What is behind that purpose is formless, but is the source of all forms. It is the force symbolised by the Maya god Itzamná.

☆ When you feel a sense of completion with the process, take a few deep breaths, and become aware of your surroundings again. When you are ready, your eyes will come open naturally.

Conclusion

The closer we study ancient civilisations, the more the realisation dawns that we know very little of our past history as a species. Certain cultures are better documented – Greece and Rome for example – but before 1000 BC relatively little is known about any of them. Even with the intensively studied civilisations such as Egypt, there are huge unknown areas. Across the 3,000 years of Egyptian culture, at least 90 per cent is still a complete blank. We aren't even certain when some of the pharaohs reigned, much less about social attitudes, the personal experiences of everyday people, their hopes, fears, and dreams, the raw material of civilisation.

Even where scholarship has been intense, there has been a tendency not to see the whole, the interaction of humans everywhere, with each other. To be fair to archaeologists and anthropologists, there is a lack of obvious evidence in most cases, though that has led many professionals to the conclusion that humanity, for most of its existence, lived in relatively isolated groups. Although there have been huge migrations of people throughout man's history, it has been believed that interchanges in ancient times were limited to land, and only occurred by sea to a very minor degree. Only recently have such assumptions been challenged. Thor Heyerdahl's journey on the raft *Kon Tiki* in the 1940s was the first real crack in the iron-clad proposition that ocean crossings were impossible. Others such as Gene Savoy have followed in their various ways.

Today a number of books, largely written by non-scientists, propose that not only was ancient man capable of long-distance connection across the seas, but that it was, if not common, not infrequent. The disdain of the 'professionals' is predictable. You are not awarded a PhD by disagreeing with orthodoxy. But it perhaps forms the opening of another crack. Without a doubt some of the ideas in these books stretch certain points a long way indeed, but the suggestion requires serious consideration.

The Maya Prophecy is a case in point.

We have traced the Prophecy and its connected messages through its arrival in Mesoamerica, speculated on some of its possible origins, have seen how the Maya sought it out, or at least sought out the knowledge of which it was part and parcel, brought it to their homeland, and built a culture around it. It powerfully emphasises how potent the original message must have been for all of this to have taken place, especially as it meshed perfectly with the past experiences of the Maya or their predecessors. It is still as potent today.

At the start, we raised four questions: What is the Prophecy? Is it true? Does it apply to you? What do you do about it? The first three have been answered as fully as possible, given the historical, geological, astronomical, and archaeological information available. It appears that the Prophecy is indeed true, and to some degree it applies to everyone.

But let's step back a moment to another statement made at

the opening of the book: that the Maya Prophecy is neither Maya nor prophecy. We have clearly demonstrated that the Prophecy existed long before the Maya. But how can we maintain that the Prophecy isn't really prophecy? As we use the word in the modern world, 'prophecy' implies seeing or foretelling the future. This is far from its original historic meaning. The essential quality of a prophet in biblical terms was not foreseeing the future, but serving as a human spokesman of a god. As the term originally came to be used, this almost invariably meant Yahweh, the God of Israel. The prophet was therefore a transmitter of divine messages, which might or might not concern future events.

There is another important distinction. A genuine prophet in the classical use of the term not only brings through messages from the god, or a foretelling of the future, but in combining these things the message must also have an ethical content. And in true prophecy the holy spirit might arrive or it might not, its appearance beyond the control of the prophet. Another difference between prophets and other 'seers' is that the soothsayer or medium in ancient times achieved their 'insights' through the use of special techniques. Diviners used dream interpretation and omen reading. Even the oracle at Delphi, who was supposedly possessed by Apollo, put herself into a trance state through the use of drugs. In the original use of the term, these lie outside the biblical definition.

When we refer to the Maya Prophecy, an essential element is absent. This removes it from the category of prophecy and firmly establishes it in the realm of prediction: what is to occur will do so regardless of human intervention. There is no moral judgement here. No change of behaviour or amount of sacrifice will prevent what is foretold, despite Maya efforts to the contrary.

This is an important distinction, because it underlines yet again the relevancy of the Prophecy – it is not dependent on a potentially dubious 'prophet' as an intermediary. Prophets of doom often spring up around a new millennium. At the end of the last millennium, the Second Coming was widely prophesied, and many of the wealthy gave away all their money and goods and retired to monasteries, only to meet a mixture of relief and disappointment in the following year. And not a few hardships. 'Earth Changes' books and literature abound in the United States, promoting all manner of geological improbabilities. In the 20th century genuine prophets such as Edgar Cayce and Paul Solomon saw important and dramatic changes just into the new millennium. We need to be careful about what we choose to believe. Taking the Prophecy out of the realm of prophecy and into the firmer stuff of 'prediction' is a big step forward.

But doesn't the fact that a catastrophe is going to happen anyway add a degree of despair? It is far from being as hopeless as it may seem. Many factors offer much hope. The most important message from the past, is that if these are indeed impact events, they are not extinction events. There is no evidence that any species has disappeared solely as a result of an impact event within the period of the Five Suns. The mammoths did finally disappear of course, but not until they were hunted to extinction by humans.

One thing central to every catastrophe or flood story is that there is a warning. Its source may be speculated on endlessly. There were human survivors in every civilisation where the warning was heeded, in whatever form it came. Of course, there would probably have been no survivors to record the story where the warning was ignored. Most ancient civilisations were built in low-lying areas near watercourses or seas. Most of the impact of the flood relates to the after-effects of the impact, and not to the impact itself. With adequate warning, many of these effects can be ameliorated.

Precisely how many of the flood stories actually occurred within the civilisations that recorded them is open to question. We have stories of horrible floods in modern times, such as the Johnstown flood in the United States in the 1920s, the massive floods in Nicaragua and Honduras in 1998. If we lived in a culture where such happenings were believed to be the work of, and the wrath of, God, we would interpret them quite differently. As survivors straggled into unaffected places bringing their stories, they might well be incorporated into the local culture. Following large-scale catastrophes in the past, the majority of people have either been unaffected, or experienced survivable hardships. It is, perhaps, 'the end of the world' for a few, but only for a few.

It is clearly demonstrated that the best hope of survival is to make the inner shifts necessary to align one's self with the patterns of nature. Even for those unable or unwilling to make the inner breakthrough back to that point of connection, all is still not lost. For the first time there actually exist technological solutions. It is even possible that it is what our compulsive drive to develop technology has actually been *for*. Some will see this as a let-off for the need to take personal and inner action to reharmonise with nature. It would be a great mistake to believe that. The technological solution is just a *possibility*.

One of the exercises in this book underlines the necessity for a heroic approach to life. It is what all the great teachers have taught in one form or another, and it is reflected in the example of the worldwide mythical archetypes that appear in every culture. The greatest act of heroism is to face ourselves – our deepest fears and insecurities – and to do what is necessary to resolve them. They are ultimately the manifestations of whatever keeps us separated from the Source of our own Being. The final purpose of all of our lives is to complete the task of reunion with our Source, whatever name we give It. When we have come such a great distance away from that Source, it can become difficult to hear the small inner voice calling us back. It is as if that voice must be raised to a shout for us to hear the message.

The Maya understood a fundamental truth of living on the Earth: all of life is a duality. The Maya Prophecy, too, must be seen in that light. What appears to be an impending catastrophe of immense proportions can actually be a benefit of the greatest consequence. It is, perhaps, the shout of the universe, calling us to inner Reunion. Given the state that much of humanity has come to, it may be the only way for the message to be heard.

Further Reading

Coe, Michael, *The Maya*, Thames and Hudson, 1993

Danielou, Alain, *The Myths and Gods of India*, Inner Traditions International, 1991

Davis, Nigel, *The Ancient Kingdoms of Mexico*, Penguin, 1990

Emery, W. B., *Archaic Egypt*, Penguin, 1987

Ginzber, Ewis, *The Legends of the Jews*, vol. 1, Jewish Publication Society of America, 1988

Hancock, Graham, *Fingerprints of the Gods*, Mandarin, 1995

Henderson, John, *The World of the Ancient Maya*, John Murray, 1997

McCleish, Kenneth, *Myth*, Bloomsbury, 1996

Morley, Sylvanus Griswold, *An Introduction to the Study of Maya Hieroglyphics*, Dover Publications, 1975

Sullivan, William, *The Secret of the Incas*, Crown, 1996

Tedlock, Dennis (trans.), *The Popul Vuh*, Simon and Schuster, 1996

Tompkins, Peter, *Mysteries of the Mexican Pyramids*, Thames and Hudson, 1987

Velikovsky, Immanuel, *Worlds in Collision*, Doubleday, 1955

Willis, Roy (ed.), *World Mythology*, BCA, 1993

Index

Piatkus Guides, written by experts, combine background information with practical exercises, and are designed to change the way you live. Titles include:

Tarot Cassandra Eason

Tarot's carefully graded advice enables readers to obtain excellent readings from Day One. You will quickly gain a thorough knowledge of both Major and Minor Arcanas and their symbolism, and learn how to use a variety of Tarot spreads.

Meditation Bill Anderton

Meditation covers the origins, theory and benefits of meditation. It includes over 30 meditations and provides all the advice you need to mediate successfully.

Crystal Wisdom Andy Baggott and Sally Morningstar

Crystal Wisdom is a fascinating guide to the healing power of crystals. It details the history and most popular modern uses of crystals and vibrational healing. It also covers colour, sound and chakra healing, and gem, crystal and flower essences.

Celtic Wisdom Andy Baggott

Celtic Wisdom is a dynamic introduction to this popular subject. The author covers Celtic spirituality, the wisdom of trees, animals and stones, ritual and ceremony and much more.

Feng Shui Jon Sandifer

Feng Shui introduces the origins, theory and practice of the Chinese art of perfect placement, or geomancy. It provides easy-to-follow techniques to help you carry out your own readings and create an auspicious living space.

The Essential Nostradamus Peter Lemesurier

The Essential Nostradamus charts the life of this extraordinary man, and includes newly discovered facts about his life and work. Peter Lemesurier unravels his prophecies for the coming decades.

Psychic Awareness Cassandra Eason

Psychic Awareness is a fascinating guide to using the power of your mind to enhance your life. Simple exercises will develop your abilities in clairvoyance, telepathy, detecting ghosts, dowsing and communicating with a spirit guide.

Reiki Penelope Quest

Reiki explains the background to this healing art and how it can improve your physical health and encourage personal and spiritual awareness and growth. Discover how simple Reiki is to use, whether for self-healing or treating other people.

Kabbalah Paul Roland

Kabbalah is an accessible guide to the origins, principles and beliefs of this mystical tradition. It includes original meditations and visualisations to help you gain higher awareness and understanding.

Colour Healing Pauline Wills

Colour Healing explains the vital role colour plays in your physical, emotional and spiritual well-being and how it is used in healing. Meditations and practical exercises will help you to discover the vibrational energies of all the colours of the rainbow.

Tibetan Buddhism Stephen Hodge

Tibetan Buddhism explains the basic teachings and central concepts of Tibetan Buddhism. There is also guidance on basic meditation, the nature of offerings and worship, and the requirements for embarking on Tantric practice.

Maya Prophecy Dr Ronald Bonewitz

Maya Prophecy is an intriguing introducting to the prophetic warnings for the future from one of the greatest early civilisations. It explores how Maya religion, mathematics and the Maya calendar provide support for the veracity of the prophecy, and how you should prepare for what lies ahead.